Walk

MW01136064

Shadow

The Story of Changing Gaits

By: Diane Ganzer

A portion of the proceeds from the sale of this book
will benefit Changing Gaits, so that they may
continue their ministry with others.
You may contact them at:
Changing Gaits
27274 Monument Road
Brook Park, MN 55007
320-679-4468
Email: info@changinggaitsinc.com
Visit www.changinggaitsinc.com

Avid Readers Publishing Group
Lakewood, California

Walking in God's Shadow

Avid Readers Publishing Group

http://www.avidreaderspg.com

ISBN-13: 978-1-935105-21-3

Printed in the United States

Acknowledgements

Special thanks goes to Guy Kaufman for sharing so much of himself, his passion for life and his love for God with others. Most important, thank you to our Lord, for giving us the strength to pick ourselves up and continue onwards, even when the odds are stacked against us. Thank you also for Shadow. If not for that amazing horse, this dream would never have materialized.

Dedication

This book is dedicated to all those who are fighting the good fight, despite adversity. May you be strengthened and grow in the love of God.

This book is also dedicated to St. Francis of Assisi. Let's not forget his prayer:

"Lord, make me an instrument of Your peace.
Where there is hatred, let me sow love;
where there is injury, pardon;
where there is doubt, faith;
where there is despair, hope;
where there is darkness, light;
where there is sadness, joy;
O Divine Master, grant that I may not so much seek to be consoled as to console;
to be understood as to understand;
to be loved as to love.
For it is in giving that we receive;
it is in pardoning that we are pardoned;
and it is in dying that we are born to eternal life!"

Sometimes Christians are called to turn the world upside down, to bring the exact opposite of what we find in our world. St. Francis' prayer is a bold one, asking for strength to **give of ourselves to meet the needs of others**. He recognizes that it "is in giving that we receive", that as we give of ourselves, we receive the peace and blessing of our risen Lord Jesus.

This is the story of Changing Gaits.

Other books by Diane Ganzer:

Patrick the Wayward Setter

A Christmas Miracle

Summer School Blues

Called to Serve

And with Sammy St Croix:

Steel Destiny

Trail Boss: The Quest

Hope Survives

Llama Tails: Ricky's Adventure

Because of Friday

Destination: Unknown!

Visit www.writeinyourearproductions.com

The most perfect early November day calls for a trail ride!

Saddle up!

Meet Akita with Guy, who makes sure she is cinched and ready

to ride while Sandy the dog awaits the chance to follow along

on this journey! Sandy, the gal atop Dozer, patiently waits to

move along!

Walking in God's

Shadow

"…Yea, though I walk through the valley of the Shadow of Death, I fear no evil, for thy rod and thy staff, they comfort me…" -Psalm 23

The prayer tree

Introduction

"For with God, nothing is impossible." -Luke 1:37

I was born into an abusive family. My mom, her mom and maybe her mother before her, all were a link in the chain which I successfully broke. However, I was still tied to the after effects of that abuse. I married an abuser and stuck through that marriage for twenty five years before finally breaking away.

I then took up a relationship for two years with an alcoholic, who was a seven time DUI offender. I enabled him, I was codependent on him. My world crashed when he was arrested for violating the terms of his probation. I was alone, scared and unsure of how to handle it. I was a "fixer," in that I wanted to help people, I wanted to be needed! I had to be in control, because I never had control all my life. When that relationship failed, due to not only the arrest, but the fact that he cut me from his life, I felt desperate. I had to find someone else NOW! I was looking for my knight in shining armor, one who would support me, yet one that I could nurture.

The next man I met seemed, at first, like my answer to that prayer I uttered. He was good looking, seemed compassionate, loved to write, as do I. I fell in love immediately. Or, I should say, I *allowed* myself to fall in love, or was it *"in need?"*

My mistake.

He was no different than my exhusband. Highly critical, stubborn to a fault. Wanting no help from me at all. Was controlling, too controlling, in fact. For two months, I did everything I could, literally "buying his love," for lack of a better term, to gain his approval, all to no avail. I bent over so far backward, I was literally kissing my own butt. He couldn't even respond in kind when I told him I loved him. Instead, it scared him too much. He finally told me he couldn't handle it, the drama of being with me. He pulled the plug on our relationship.

Does codependent mean *anything* to me? When he broke up with me, it was almost a relief. I had been walking on eggshells with him, too afraid to say "boo." He didn't like for me to cry. He never cried either, he bragged. His sense of humor was way off. He did marijuana. He came from a family with an alcoholic dad, whose issues were never resolved before his father passed on. He shunned churches, saying they were for hypocrites. I could go on forever, but needless to say, once more, I had tried to change him, hoping that my goodness would rub off on him. It had the opposite effect. He resisted my efforts. Due to his attitude about church, I also pulled back from it. I wanted him to "love me," remember?

Unfortunately, my anxiety with this relationship affected my seventeen year old daughter more than I knew. She melted down one day, screaming at me, "can't you see, mom? He's USING you! You're nothing more than his *fuck buddy!* He's no different than dad or Sammy was!" (referring to my last two relationships.) She refused to speak with me after that.

I was shocked! The word, "but...but...but..." kept going through my head. "But, I can still change him, I know I can!" Coincidentally, it was just two days later that he referred to her, out of the blue, as "your fuckin' daughter." Such compassion!

My daughter saw something I that couldn't, in my codependent state, see: he was using me. There was no love on his part. None. How could he love anyone, when he himself came from a troubled background? He didn't know how to love either. I knew then, I had to save myself, as well as my relationship with my daughter, for hell has no fury like a mom who needs to protect her daughter from this spasm of hatred that he had spewed at her, and she had done nothing to deserve it.

When I met Guy at Changing Gaits, I immediately felt the love that he has for God, for humanity, for animals. I first came to him to interview him for my weekly radio program. Two weeks later, I stopped out to his ranch to take some serious "me time," to heal. Little did I know how transforming that day would be.

Guy took me to his barn, where he had a course all set up in the arena. There were a series of obstacles in a circle that looked like a pathway. Guy told me to choose a horse, which I did. He then told me to choose a path, which I did. Then he told me to name the obstacles in my way. I was codependent. BIG hurdle. So, in effect, the horse became that codependency and my mission was to navigate the horse, by holding the lead in one hand, and leading it through the obstacles, without going over the preset path. As soon as I was between the first obstacle, which represented my fear of abandonment, and the second, which represented my fear of never finding someone to love me, the horse, named Dozer, suddenly stopped, stepping on the middle of the lead. I looked at Dozer. He looked back at me almost knowingly. I asked him to release his foot from the lead so that we could continue.

He didn't.

I pulled hard on the lead.

No avail.

Once more, I looked at the horse. In that second, his eyes were looking not at me, but THROUGH me, I knew then that God was showing me Himself, through this horse!
God knew of my pain, my suffering through so many hurts in my life, my fears of abandonment, my dashed hopes.

Guy then gently asked me what it was that I wanted to do.

I replied, "to let go of my codependency."

He told me to unhook the lead from the horse. As soon as I did, Dozer meandered to the far side of the arena, to munch on hay. I was then able to navigate the other obstacles, naming them as I went, surprised at how easy it was, now that "codependency" was no longer attached to me. When I made it past the last obstacle, I walked over and looked up--at the CROSS of Christ! "Why didn't I see that before," I asked, awestruck.

"Because," Guy replied, "it was your perception of things. You thought you could do it all alone, and you left God out. You only saw obstacles. Now you see that God was there all along.

And look also, at the path you've chosen."

I did, and was stunned. I had chosen the narrow path!

"Not many choose the narrow path," Guy said, "but as you can see, the other, wider path, leads to…" and he pointed out, it lead straight to nowhere! The narrow one lead straight to God.

"Narrow is the road and few are the ones finding it. You have chosen the road less traveled and made all the better for it."

I put my hands over my face and cried, releasing so many hurts.

Was I instantly healed? No, that is a process that will take time, but looking back there, at the obstacles I passed, I realized that my life was slowly healing. I went from an abusive twenty five year marriage, to a two year relationship with an alcoholic to a two month relationship with my last "boyfriend," the one that I thought would care for me forever. Now I know, I need to care for myself, to enable MYSELF to be one with God.

In retrospect, my boyfriend was so consumed with himself, his desires, that he had no room in his life for anyone, he had bragged, let alone God. But I also realized that my relationships with these codependents were becoming less in the duration of time, from twenty five years to just two months. I was learning what I should and should not have to tolerate to have a happy relationship. I was making progress, and we only learn by doing.

"...and lest the greatness of the revelations should puff me up, the was given to me a thorn for the flesh, a messenger of Satan, to buffet me. Concerning this, three times I sought the Lord, that it might leave me. And he said to me, "My grace is sufficient for you, for strength is made perfect in weakness. Gladly therefore, I will carry my infirmities, that the strength of Christ may dwell in me. Wherefore, I am satisfied, for Christ's sake, with infirmities, with insults, with hardships, with persecutions, with distresses, FOR WHEN I AM WEAK, THEN I AM STRONG!"

-2 Corinthians 12:7-10

There are many more stories such as this that you are about to read. I have always said that every person's life touches so many other lives. The next story that I will tell you is one of pain, but also, one of hope. It is about Changing Gaits founder, Guy Kaufman. He is a work in progress and his life IS touching so many other lives in very positive ways!

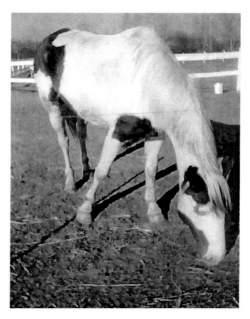

Diesel

Chapter One - Guy's Story

"I can do everything through Him that gives me strength"
Philippians 4:1

How would you define insanity, and how is that stopping you from achieving your purpose in life?

One could say that insanity is doing the same thing, the same way, over and over again, expecting different results, yet the outcome always remains the same.

1

Raised Catholic in in St. Paul, MN in the 1960's, Guy knew little about horses other than "Silver" from the Lone Ranger and others highlighted in TV shows. He began abusing alcohol as a teenager to numb himself from family problems. His wake up call came Labor Day weekend in 1998 at a lakeside cabin in western Wisconsin. He emerged from an alcoholic stupor, realizing that he could not account for three days or how his son had spent them. Ashamed, he tried to walk in front of an oncoming semi on a darkened road that night. The truck narrowly missed him.

The near miss was an epiphany.

"I was sick and tired of being sick and tired," Guy recalls.

Oh, how many of us can identify with that! It was no different with me and my codependent relationships! As long as I had someone to "care for," who maybe, if I bought enough attention, would say the magic words I longed to hear, I could be so "happy!" Yet for all my attempts, I always wound up being hurt in the end! "Why?" I'd scream at God! "What do I have to do to *make* someone love me?"

See the definition of insanity here? People love you

because of who you *are,* not what you *do* for them. It's a long journey, but when you grow up unloved and unworthy, what price would you pay to have some semblance of positive attention in your life? For me, it was many dollars spent keeping my men happy by buying them everything their heart desired…booze! CD's! Computers! The list goes on forever, and in the end, what did I have to show for it, except thousands of dollars of credit card debt, an empty heart and a cold bed at night. Those men have moved on, more comfortable, thanks to…me.

Such insanity!

The miracle for Guy came in the form of an Arabian horse named "Shadow." Guy met Shadow at the Wild River Stables in Chisago Lakes. Guy was barely a year into recovery, with the temptation to relapse always a constant in his life. Riding Shadow gave Guy a different kind of high.

"That first day, we rode a three hour trail in forty five minutes," Guy said. "It was a great sense of serenity, peace and purpose riding him." This lead to Guy quitting the meter reader job he had and working at the stables as a horse riding guide- no salary involved. His reward a few years later was in owning Shadow.

Shadow saved Guy's life at that point, he gave the man his purpose in life.

Guy also saved Shadow's life. In a freak accident, Shadow's neck became tightly caught in twine, literally suffocating the horse. Several vets suggested putting the horse down. Guy would have none of that. He turned to the One he knew would save his beloved horse, his faith like that of a mustard seed which has always been known to move mountains. In time, Shadow slowly recovered. Guy saw this as an omen.

After a bout of kidney stones, eighteen in fact, Guy's addictive personality wouldn't let him take pain medications. Lying in incredible pain, he questioned God, "what do you want me to do in my life?" He felt a compelling voice, whispering to him. "Horses and kids, horses and kids," pounding into his senses. After reading the book "The Dream Giver," by Bruce Wilkinson, Multnomah Books, he realized that God was calling him. He was changed.

Witnessing a seminar in Tennessee known as EAGALA-Equine Assisted Growth and Learning Association- a nationally recognized therapy outfit based in Santaquin, Utah, Guy became excited, as the bells and whistles went off in his head, he realized that this is what he was saved for… the addictions, the two suicide attempts, the despair at ever finding his journey in life were preparing him for this moment.

"Do you see? Nothing is rationed to you, beloveds. Whatever you have a lot of, you can have more. Where I am, there are no limits. The same can be said for you and where you are. The only limits are those that you perceive and accept. No longer accept limits- the sky is not even the limit. Does that mean that everything will be just as you desire it to be? No, but it does mean that there is no ceiling on you. Going for what you want is your achievement! No matter what, you are contributing to life in the world. What would you like to do? What is meaningful to you? That is your contribution. All you really need to know is that you are destined for a journey in life."
from heavenletters.org 8/16/08

This doesn't mean that everything came easy for Guy from that point on. Absolutely not!

Every day is one step forward, taken in a world where it is so easily to fall backwards by three. Yet Guy persisted, doors opened and Changing Gaits was born in June 2004. Guy himself is a Certified Equine Specialist through EAGALA. The motto at Changing Gaits is "horses… healing… changing lives, body, mind and soul." Using Equine Assisted Addiction services, it is a collaborative effort between a licensed alcohol and drug counselor and an equine specialist who work together to design sessions that require the client to apply certain skills. The process is intense but effective and compliments other treatment options.

Participants in the program learn about themselves and others by participation in activities with horses; a dynamic and powerful living being, using skills such as non-verbal communication, creative thinking and problem solving.

Why horses, you ask? Those familiar with horses have long recognized and understood their power and influence on people. Horses are large and powerful, which creates a natural opportunity to overcome fear and develop confidence while working with them, providing metaphors to use when dealing with other intimidating and challenging situations in life.

Horses are excellent at reading our body language and will respond to it honestly, which makes them powerful messengers. They are able to read and mirror body language. This creates a situation that requires us as humans to rethink our approach with them and try to communicate in a different manner.

If you remember in the introduction, Dozer stepped on the lead as I was leading him around the obstacles. My attempts to get him off the lead worked only when I was able to unsnap the lead and set him free. He represented my codependency. The interesting thing was the way he looked me in the eye as I was trying to "make a deal" with him, afraid to really be firm and speak up about my request to step off the rope! The same occurred when I was on the trail with him awhile later. I had to keep in mind that he was my "codependency" as well there. I had to be firm, to rein him in as needed, to *not* allow his way of thinking dictate where *I* would be lead. To allow myself to trust in *myself*!

How often did I let *men* tell *me* what to do, where to go and how high to jump, subconsciously holding out their "love" for me until I gave in to their needs, wants and demands. I was enabling them to be the selfish people they were, with no thought as to what I also wanted. Not a healthy situation by any means. I deserve to be loved, I deserve to be respected, it is my right!

"My help comes from the Lord, the Maker of heaven and earth." -Psalm 121:2

As Guy has found out, as I am finding out and so many others who either have been through treatment or are undergoing it, we cannot do it alone. You need to trust in God to be able to face each day, because to do it alone is almost a recipe for disaster.

Here is a testimonial from a gal who also has been through the program at Changing Gaits.

Akita

Chapter Two - Sarah's Story

"For I know the plans I have for you," declares the Lord, "Plans to prosper you and not to harm you, plans to give you a hope and a future." -Jeremiah 29:11

"What are the barriers between you and GOD?" (Good, Orderly Direction)

Diane Ganzer

From a testimony received 1/26/2008 at Changing Gaits…

"I'm not sure what made me stand out or how God chose me, but the fact that I still have breath in my tortured body today confirms one powerful message: I am here for his greater purpose. In high school, I was happy healthy and had a hopeful future ahead of me. I excelled in sports, I had a responsible job, a scholarship to Kansas State University, took exceptional care of my American Quarter horse, I was full of life and had a carefree spirit.

"I was 18 when it all happened. I was at my friend's house when his father walked into the hallway naked. We were in utter shock but laughed it off. It was while I was sleeping that I felt his hand on me.

"I was never the same after that. I became a different person, a person I didn't recognize. I suffered from post traumatic stress disorder and became deeply involved in an unhealthy, codependent relationship with a drug user/alcoholic. I was hardly concerned for my own virtue and I was usually detached from my own emotions What little respect I had for my body left me panic stricken only because of what I had given away physically. I felt

10

dirty, used, taken advantage of. I thought I was a whore, yet I didn't know how to say, 'no.'

"My high school senior year was a struggle, because I lived two lives. I still excelled while hiding my pain. Because of the abuse, conflict arose, I was considered a liar by some of the people from that party and long term friendships were destroyed. I lived in guilt because I had thought it was all my fault. The sense of belonging that I had was approaching an end. My sense of identity was lost and I didn't know who I was becoming. My boyfriend relapsed into drugs and our relationship ended. I was left with an emptiness more than I could bear, I developed an eating disorder.

"The obsession wrapped itself around me constantly. I began counting calories and was constantly moving. The sight of a loaf of bread was overwhelming. I was controlling and irritable. I dropped weight and was considered anorexic. My pulse rate was in the 30's, I was weak and tired. I went to a dietician, yet continued bingeing and over exercising. Then came the overuse of laxatives as a way to purge rather than by over exercising. I attempted suicide by taking an overdose of pills. I spent five months in a residential treatment facility in Texas and there

met Chris Kaufman through phone conversations and letters. I was interested in becoming a certified horse specialist; Chris suggested that I speak with his father, Guy. With much fear, I made that call to a complete stranger, expressing my interest in visiting Changing Gaits to see what the program was all about. I was struck by that three letter word that Guy used which I knew nothing about:

"God.

"Impulsively, I took a weekend trip to Minnesota, meeting with Guy and all the horses I had heard so much about. I was fascinated, Changing Gaits was like a breath of fresh air! Despite all my inner turmoil, I could breathe here. There was a peace and serenity about the place that made me feel invited and at home. Even during a time when I had no concept about God, I could sense this was a place where miracles were created. Located on seventy seven gorgeous acres in the heart of Brook Park, Minnesota, just south of Hinckley, it is literally paradise!

Guy welcomed me with a light, loving heart and a warm accepting smile.

"The bulimia spun out of control. I was taking so many laxatives that I was throwing up and fainting. I was abusing them

daily and yet still gaining weight due to the excessive binging. I felt the suicidal desperation again. I would rather have died than gained weight anymore. I hung a rope in my mom's basement and began to choke myself with it just to get a feel for the real thing. I was planning on hanging myself in her garage. I went to the psychiatric hospital yet again where I spent Thanksgiving and a total of nine days. I ended up failing most of the classes I was enrolled in. I was no longer excelling, I was barely even getting by. I was insane. Suicidal thoughts ran through my head daily. I knew that if I binged to a certain point, the pain would become so intolerable that I would push myself over the edge. I believed that my eating disorder was going to kill me, once I became miserable enough, I would have the courage to take my own life. I talked to Chris on the phone. I said that my parents were unavailable to help me financially so treatment was not an option. All I had was an SSI disability check, which I received due to my inability to hold down a job.

"Changing Gaits let me come even in my brokenness.

"I came to Changing Gaits knowing everything about horses, yet little about myself. During my first session, I shared my story about being sexually abused. Moments later, I was given

the task to elect my therapy horse. To my astonishment, I chose the only mare in a pasture full of geldings. I favored a mare unintentionally and claimed that I selected her because I felt she was safe. Akita, a beautiful buckskin mare had also been abused. She has a scar on her back from where she was beaten with a steel pipe. Akita and I had an unusual bond. She rarely trusted anyone, yet she followed me around the arena without the aid of a lead rope, and she enjoyed cantering on the trails while I rode on her bare back. Through Akita, Guy and Cheryl could see my strengths and weaknesses. I began using the horses to set healthy boundaries. I was able to tell Orion 'no' and physically move away from him when he invaded my personal space. I practiced telling Akita, Cinnamon and a miniature horse named Ginger that 'I deserve love and respect.' Eventually I was able to tell Guy and Cheryl that 'I deserve love and respect' too.

"Guy taught me that I needed to build spiritual armor in order to protect myself from the devil. That armor consisted of a strong support group, the Good *Orderly Direction of God and the Bible, receiving it while at Changing Gaits. Guy used an acronym to describe the Bible as the Basic Instructions Before Leaving the Earth. He surrounded me with other Christians who*

loved me even though I hated myself.

"*I returned home before I was ready to. My spirituality, which had been so fragile to develop, was soon blocked once more by the eating disorder. I was knocked down harder than ever before. I isolated myself completely for two whole months, lying to my friends, telling them I was out of town in order to avoid them. I binged day in and day out. I ran out of money so I stole from my family. The were angry, so I stole from the grocery store. I felt a level of helplessness and desperation which was far greater than before. If I wasn't passed out from a drastic drop in blood pressure, I was bingeing. I only left the house once a day to go steal from the grocery store. I sometimes would wake up from my carb-coma screaming, then slap myself across the face, pulling out my hair. I hated myself for being so out of control. There was nothing left and I knew this was the intolerable pain that would push me over the edge. Late at night, I would get on the internet and research how to tie a noose. I learned how long the rope had to be to accommodate my weight in order to insure that my head would snap. I drove to the train tracks and fantasize about leaping in front of the train's path.*

"*It was around 9:30 PM November 13th when I decided I*

was going to do it.

"I was going to end my suffering. I didn't want to leave a note, but I did want to say goodbye to Guy. I hadn't talked to him for nearly three months. When he answered the phone, I was immediately comforted by the sound of his voice. I explained what was going on. I was distressed, hyperventilating and couldn't stop crying. Guy's expressions calmed me down so that I could breathe again. I became saturated in his words and I understood for the first time that I am surviving for a reason. I had ingested 80-100 pills earlier, surviving. I woke up on my own, no mystery as to how: it was God. I felt an impulse to go to Minnesota in order to watch a demonstration conducted by a complete stranger. I can't explain what on earth would possess me to leave so abruptly: it was God. The fact that Chris and my friend Sara gave me the Changing Gaits brochure was not an act of random kindness, it was God!

"Still on the phone, Guy told me that as long as I was still alive, there is still hope. Even though I feel that I am too far gone to pull myself back up, as long as I am still breathing, God has a reason for it. Right there, sitting in my car, my life changed. I had been on my way to the train tracks for the last time, but after I

hung up the phone with Guy, I decided to do something different. I decided that I am going to live my life, one day at a time, for the glory of Jesus Christ.

"Since that night, things have changed. I left the next morning and went to a psychiatric hospital, which I had never been to before. The hospital staff connected me with a new outpatient team. I have become more confident in myself and have been assertive during situations I would have lost my voice during the past. Guy convinced me that I have this disease for a reason; to help other people who may be struggling as well. I hope to be able to pass on what Guy has taught me. Guy offered everything he had to me. I did nothing to deserve it and he asked for nothing in return. We are all put upon this earth to fulfill a temporary assignment. Nothing is ours, we are merely borrowing objects from God as trusts. We are create in God's image to become like Christ; self sacrificing and selfless. I cannot portray Guy as any other way. In the midst of my brokenness, Guy saw my strengths. He made me feel important by giving me jobs with the horses and allowing me to expand on my talents. His ability to relate to people and uncover their buried emotions in a gentle way is a God-given gift. His love for Jesus Christ radiates

through him and inspires those around him. Guy speaks of Jesus night and day and appears to read the Bible even in his sleep. My spiritual family may be in Minnesota, but I take Jesus in my heart, wherever I go. I am no longer alone. I found the missing piece, which brings about my recovery. I wouldn't trade all that I have been through because it led me to where I am today. Changing Gaits is a miracle from God."

"For it is God who works in you to will and to act according to his good purpose."

-Philippians 2:13

Chapter Three - In His Own Words

"Therefore, I urge you brothers, in view of God's mercy, to offer your bodies as living sacrifices, holy and pleasing to God- this is your spiritual act of worship."- Romans 12:1

Which of your behaviors surprised you- and why?

"Lord, tell me your ways, show me how to live Guide me in Your truth and teach me, my God and Savior. I trust you all day long."
-Psalm 25:4

Guy's story

  "I came from abusive family, mom had been beaten by dad as were us kids. They divorced when I was about 14 years

old. Mom raised four kids, dad saw them on weekends, when they watched football together. I drank through high school to medicate from the pain. I remember the shame I felt when I made a clay handprint in school. On the way home, it broke in several pieces. Picking up those pieces, I took it home to show my mom.

"Oh, it probably wasn't that good anyway," she had said. I also remember the isolation I felt, wearing huge "coke bottle lens" glasses, due to having weak eyesight. The pain of being called four eyes. It continued to build, each painful memory on the last, until angry, bitter and resentful I began to drink. I vividly remember, after a party, vomiting all over my favorite set of baseball cards. They had to be thrown away. I was on probation from St Bernard's school for drinking, but never had a DWI or accident related to drinking in my life.

In 1989, I gave up drinking for five years, but never sought treatment. What got me started again was a series of events; my then wife goaded me to "have a beer," beginning a cycle that brought strain on the marriage due to her affair, as also did an assault, in which I had too do fifty hours of community service. That was a good thing, because my kids got to see their dad feeding the homeless people in St Paul Also what continued my drinking was dealing with the stress when my dad died, and I was served divorce papers. By then, I was tired of life, attempting suicide not once but twice. The first time I was on a catwalk at work looking down, a long way down, to my doom on the concrete below. I was saved by a friend, who pulled me back. The second time, which was more horrific, I was camping in Shell Lake, WI with my kids. For several days, I went on a binge. My attitude at an all time low, I picked a fight with someone who was taller but less muscular than I was while at a bar. For no reason at all, I popped him such a hard punch, it impacted everyone else at the bar as they crashed into one another. Like a scene from an old TV western, I waited for the inevitable smack back. I wanted it, I yearned for it. "Take me out," I thought, "I'm waiting." It didn't happen. I then left the bar, deliberately stumbling right in front of a semi truck. The truck swerved to miss me, I rolled down an embankment leading to the lake itself. There I puked all over myself. Going back to my camper, I had the shakes so bad. My own son, disgusted with me, refused to speak to me. "Who's that kid you're with, the one with the long hair?" I snarled at him.

*"He's **their** son!" Chris had said, pointing out the friends that were also with them. Chris then retorted back, "Where've*

you been all weekend, dad?"

If that wasn't a wake up call, nothing would have snapped him out of it.

"It was then," Guy remembers, "that I was sick and tired of being sick and tired." He checked into treatment program, in which he was to write his obituary. His predicted day of death was Aug 31. Angry, he hurled epithets at the counselor, only then realizing...she was right. He got serious about recovery, attending 90 meetings in 90 days.

It was also time to begin a new life. He sold his home in 1999 for a tidy profit, living his life in a 20 foot Winnebago, first at William O'Brien State Park, then at Taylor's Falls and finally ending up at Wild River, where he met Hank Magnuson. Working for him as a lead guide, his dream was slowly taking root, manifesting itself, yet Guy did not know it just yet. It was Hank that helped Guy to find Jesus, by holding Bible study meetings, bolstering Guy's faith in Christ. It strengthened him for the next phase; he moved on from Wild River campground, going now to Country Camping in Isanti, MN. There he met Patty Midlo and her husband Lee, both Catholic. Lee was like an older brother to Guy, who felt right at home here. He moved there in July 1999, giving up his tiny twenty foot Winnebago for a 49 x 12 park model home, which was to be his last home before moving into Changing Gaits facilities. This campground was secure for his recovery in that it had a Twelve Step Program, a pig roast, everything to make the visitor feel welcome. Guy repaid his stay by performing lawn maintenance work for them.

He credits first Hank, then Patty and Lee, then Todd and finally Greg Koalska, in that order, for helping him to build on the whole Changing Gaits idea. "It is like building a house, and they were the foundation," he commented. "And it needed to be in that order. If not for the initial assurance from Hank, nothing Patty said or did would have mattered."

His philosophy is that he is doing Changing Gaits not for the money, but to help those who need it. "I don't want to be like my father," he emphasized. A plaque that he treasures says: "I'm not where I want to be, I'm not where I should be, but thank God I'm not where I used to be!"

It is his desire to be a shining light, as Matthew 5:14 says... *"You are the Light that gives light to the world. A city that*

Diane Ganzer

is built on a hill can't be hidden, and people don't put light under a bowl. They put it on a lamp stand so the light shines for all people to see. In the same way, you should be a light for other people. Live so they will see the good things that you do and will praise your Father in heaven."

"It is important to heal the inner child, to make peace with that little Guy from so long ago, to say, "it isn't your fault," just as it's important for the big Guy to also say to the little one, "it wasn't your fault." Then, stop replaying those scenes that hurt us," Guy continued.

Taking me into his bedroom, he points out the top of his bureau. There are ten different trophies on display, one for each year of his sobriety, given to him by his kids. Proudly, he picks up number nine. Engraved on it is the quote, "where have you been all weekend, dad?" This one represents his "missing weekend" in Shell Lake, Wisconsin. It is a constant daily reminder of just how close he came…to not being that shining light in the lives of so many others.

"Every person's life touches so many other lives," so says the quote from that holiday staple, "It's a Wonderful Life."

Indeed it is! And indeed, we do touch lives, for better…

or, as Guy found out from that lost weekend, for worse.

As Guy is relating his story to me, it is a beautiful day, late October, the wind is gently ruffling the grasses in the nearby pasture where the horses are grazing. Suddenly, with no warning, they all decided to come running towards us. I gasped, mesmerized, from the sheer beauty of eleven horses in action, one right after the other. It was no different than what one would see in a movie and the magnitude of it took my breath away.

"Oh, yeah," Guy said, laughing, "they do that a lot!"

"You are so lucky too be able to see that so much!" I gushed out.

Guy suggested that we go outside to enjoy the warm day.

The horses are grazing contentedly in the nearby pasture, several lady bugs are buzzing around the deck where we were sitting, sipping coffee and enjoying the moment.

Integrity is very important to him, to do and say what you mean, then carry that out. Case in point: A gal who went on a moonlight ride at Changing Gaits, lost several credit cards, her card key for work and two twenty dollar bills. It had been incredibly windy for the two consecutive days after her ride and

Guy doubted that he'd find anything, yet reassured her that if he did, he'd let her know. Like a miracle, the cards turned up, one here, another there. Going to his prayer tree, he lay down for a quick nap in the hammock that he has stretched across a small lean to. The sounds of the wind and the peace lulled him into slumber. Upon getting up, he was surprised to find, only ten yards from each other, the two twenty dollar bills! Now, conceivably, he could have kept that money, but instead, returned it! "I'd love to be an angel in that room when she opens that envelope and sees what's inside! That forty dollars can easily become forty thousand!" Guy recalled. "Who knows what she will say to people, but you can bet that the Lord will repay that over and over." Not even three weeks later, Guy went to the mailbox, as he does each day, praying for the miracle check that will arrive to keep the horses fed, to provide for the needs of Changing Gaits. He looked at the one card he received, then opened it up. With shaking hands he read the message as the check lay like a beacon, in his lap.

"The check is to be used as you see fit for the needs of Changing Gaits," the card read.

"Thank you, Jesus!" he uttered over and over again, tears

pouring down his face.

The check was from the gal who had lost her credit cards and the two twenty dollar bills.

It was for four....hundred...dollars. God did indeed repay, ten times over!

Guy has the satisfaction of being exactly where God has placed him. Surveying his property on this beautiful, warm late October day, giving thanks for that gift in north central Minnesota so late in the year, Guy speculated on where his project will lead. As I listened, I also heard from far away the sounds of a rooster from another farm, as well as the sounds of a pheasant coming from the opposite field.

"I envision four cottages there," he pointed to a spot in the east pasture. "Then another four over there, for the families to stay. I see a second arena out there, as well as taking the miniature horses into Catholic schools, to reach the youngsters before their problems set in, so they don't become addicts, or attempt suicide out of the desperation that I had felt. I envision several more Changing Gaits facilities, one on the East coast, one in California, one in Arizona, maybe Florida, Texas and Ohio."

One day at a time, one person at a time, one heart at a

time. That's the way to do it. "Each day is a gift," Guy said. "That's why it's the present. Praise God!"

Looking into his eager bright blue eyes, I had no doubt that his vision will take place. If you do what you love, with no thought of personal gain, miracles can happen.

God grant me the serenity to accept the things I cannot change. The courage to change the things I can and the wisdom to know the difference.

Reach high, for stars lie hidden in you.
Dream deep, for every dream precedes the goal.

RABINDRANATH TAGORE

November 10th

NANCY E. FRANK

11-10   2008

PAY TO THE
ORDER OF   Changing Gaits Inc | $ 400.00

Four Hundred   DOLLARS

FOR Horses you see fit.   Nancy Frank

You treat the horses
the way I think they
should be treated
(like family) GOD BLESS YOU.

Keep it up! Nancy Frank

Guy just a little note
to let you know that I
got your letter (I still am
amazed that you found
everything with the wind
gusting for days! (?))
Someday I'd like to bring my
elderly mother by (she's in a
wheelchair so I might have to
wait for spring) She was so
happy to know they get apples! ☺

29

Chapter Four - Shadow's Story

Shadow is a bay Arabian gelding that was residing at Wild River Stables when Guy met up with him. Shadow was just as green as Guy was, but together, they made a formidable team. On June 29, 2004, Guy went to the stable in search of Shadow, only to find him with baling twine wrapped around his throat so tight, it was nearly suffocating him.

"His head was as big as a hippopotamus," Guy recalled. "His eyes were literally bugged out of his head and blood and mucous were pouring from his nose. Guy cut the twine loose, called the vet and began praying. While waiting for the vet for forty five minutes, Guy ran to call the vet again, who had become lost and needed directions. While Guy was gone, Shadow whinnied once, what Hank Magnuson, who also was present, thought was

30

Shadow's final gasp. But Shadow hung on. In the midst of so much pain, Hank wondered why the horse would waste what precious energy it had left while Guy was at the phone.

"Well, I suppose Shadow missed me," Guy had recalled telling Hank.

Hank asked Shadow, "do you just need to be by Guy?"

Shadow shook his massively swollen head up and down five times.

At that, Hank turned his head and began to cry in amazement.

Guy knew, he couldn't let Shadow go.

When the Sunrise Equine Vet Services arrived, they said it was the worst case of strangulation they had ever seen.

The vet recommended putting Shadow down.

Immediately.

Guy refused. "You don't understand," he pleaded. "Me and Shadow, we made a deal with God to save kids. This horse ain't going *nowhere*!"

With Shadow near death, Guy insisted that the vet perform an emergency tracheotomy in the field. The vet expertly rigged a makeshift tube out of a syringe, which Guy held in place in

Shadow's throat, his hand almost disappearing inside the horse's throat during the long drive to the Stillwater vet's location.

"You're gonna make it, boy, ya hear me? We have work to do and you need to be here to do it!" Guy crooned over and over.

As if Shadow knew that he was no longer alone, he summoned the will from deep within him to continue his fight, knowing that God, who loves His creatures deeply, was whispering into his ear over and over, "you are destined for great things, this will be the first miracle of many…"

The team at the clinic concurred with the vet from Sunrise; they could not save the beloved horse, he would have to be put down.

What they didn't know was that true faith does NOT waiver under testing, in fact, it only becomes stronger!

"I want Shadow's life saved!" Guy insisted, over and over, that the vet treat Shadow. While watching the vet work, Guy began to pray.

"God, you know what it is that I need to do. If it's Your will that he lives, I will dedicate my life to Your work."

Shadow did survive, miraculously. By morning, the

horse was eating and drinking. Only ten days after the accident, Shadow was back in the stable, needing only one minor surgery afterwards.

"Mr. Kaufman, your horse is a one in one million survivor, and you got the one." The vet was absolutely astounded at the odds.

"I wonder if the other 999,999 had faith in Jesus Christ," Guy replied.

True to his word, Changing Gaits was born from this experience. Guy's friend, Todd Schilling, came forward with an offer to help build the facility for the equestrian based program. It was Todd who took Guy to his treatment sessions and stuck by him through thick and thin. It was the original plan to have Changing Gaits run as a "for profit" agency, but once again, life intervened.

Todd's dad passed on, creating an interruption of those plans.

It was when Guy was going to see a concert featuring Steven Curtis Chapman one cold December day that he ran into someone who became the key catalyst to the ongoing plans.

Greg Koalska, whose sister went to the same high school

with Guy, was at the will- call window, picking up tickets when Guy came by to get his own tickets. Guy told him all about Changing Gaits, going so far as to comment, "when you hear Steven Curtis Chapman singing, "The Great Adventure," I want you to close your eyes and think about recovery."

Mercy Me opened the concert by announcing that the songs for that show would be of the Christmas variety. Guy had thought at that point that maybe his announcement to Greg was a bit premature. But then, Mercy Me continued.

"However, we have decided, as has Steven, to perform one song from our regular set of music that we will play for you."

Sure enough, it was "The Great Adventure."

Yes, Greg had been touched by that song and wanted more information about Changing Gaits, so he spoke with Todd Schilling. At that point, due to the death of Todd's dad, the project couldn't be financed by Todd now that he had things to settle financially with his family, and yet it was Greg, who worked as an investments analyst, who paid the monthly mortgage fee to keep the project alive, making it a reality even today.

"I had the opportunity, once I found out about Changing

Gaits, to want to be a part of this vision that Guy has," Greg said. "I have been blessed and I want to pass that on, as long as I can. I want to be that light that shines for all to see."

Guy admits that Todd, Greg, Hank and Peggy are the foundation of what Changing Gaits is. Without that, there would be no supporting cast to build upon.

Starting with Shadow, the other horses began arriving, one by one. Each has had a difficult transition in it's life, many from abuse and neglect. Each horse has a past to overcome, just like the kids and adults they are helping.

Guy was joined by Cheryl Shanahan, a licensed alcohol and drug counselor who has been working in the field since 1980. Guy quickly points out that Changing Gaits is a supplement to other treatment programs, it is not meant to replace them. It serves as a means to help build self esteem and address certain aspects of addictive behavior or to reach people who may not respond to traditional treatment approaches.

As Lynn Thomas explains, "people don't change unless they are uncomfortable and people don't grow unless challenged."

Chapter Five - Diane's Story

"Let us examine our ways and test them, and let us return to the Lord." -Lamentations 3:40

Which of your behaviors would you like to see more of….or less of…and why?

One of the goals of every horse handler, whether riding or working the horse in hand, is to change gaits and direction fairly smoothly. Most horses learn to do this fairly easily with a little teaching. If only it could be this easy for us humans to make needed transitions in our lives! Thus the name, Changing Gaits!

It takes more than just education for people to change direction and overcome obstacles. For many people caught up in addiction and other destructive behaviors, it takes faith, encouragement, a belief in oneself and sometimes, a few miracles.

Do miracles happen all by themselves? It is said that God helps those who help themselves. But if one is caught up in destructive behaviors, then a gentle nudge is needed to gain control of the situation, if only to recognize it, as the last testimony related.

"Many times, I myself have stormed heaven, screaming, "God! I can't do this all alone anymore! It hurts so bad! I feel so unloved/unwanted/uncared for! Why are You so far away?"

"Maybe God isn't so far away after all, maybe it is US who moved away. God is just waiting for us to come back.

"Come back...come back..."

"When one has been beaten down time after time after time, when the same patterns have been relived over and over and over again, when the nightmares come crashing in during the day, then it is really hard to hear the small voice of God, telling us to come to Him. "Cast your burdens on Me, for my

yoke is easy and My load is light," God said.

"*My own behaviors, the compelling, almost obsessive need to "fix" people's issues, stemmed from when I was very young, growing up in an abusive family. I was told, almost daily, by my mother, how I was unwanted, unplanned for, unloved, unworthy. Yet, I was the peace keeper in my family, the moderator of my parent's fights, the advocate between my siblings, the unnagging wife, the responsible girlfriend, the reliable coworker, the helpful co-author. It was hard juggling all of those roles, oh God, so hard, yet I felt I was "accomplishing" something. I was a hero, all I needed was a pat on the back because I did so good. Right?*

"*I'm still waiting for those pats. Despite my accomplishments of always being so good, I feel unloved, unworthy, so I try even more, to produce the desired effect... remember the definition of insanity?*

"*I have broken up with that boyfriend, the previous one is in prison for his alcoholic violations of his DUI probation, my exhusband was a wife abuser. My parents are gone. What a comedown.*

"*What did I do for* **myself**? *I felt it was selfish of me to want any special treatment, it was all about the other person. I*

38

will bend so far backwards to help another, but I had forgotten…
me. If I wasn't attending to someone else, I felt lost, bereft, forlorn,
panicky even! I had to "fix" something, that was my crutch, my
"high." I could only feel good if I controlled the situation. My
last boyfriend hated that, he wanted the control and resented me
*for what I was doing for him. "I can do it all by **myself!**" he said.*
*"I always have, I don't need **you!**"*

"Unfortunately, I didn't get mad, I got even! "Don't need
me, eh?" I thought. "After all I did for you, you don't need me?
How dare you! You will remember me for the rest of your life!
I will hurt you just as you have hurt me!" And so I did. I wrote
an extremely hurtful letter, which I posted on the front page of
his website, words so spiteful that once it was seen, there was
no turning back. The trust I had built so carefully was now torn
asunder.

"Not a very Christian like attitude here! Jesus told his
followers that they were to wipe their feet of the town that refused
them, NOT to become vindictive! Yet here I was, anger coursing
through me because I was rebuffed! Satan was certainly present
in my life for me to allow such a negative feeling to take over.

"Two days later, pacing my bedroom, I cried bitter tears.

I even asked God why I was still alive. I asked him to condemn me to death right now! I was ready for His punishment.

"Why?

"Because I had failed YET again! I didn't deserve anything less than His hatred! I looked at a statue that I have of the Blessed Virgin that sat high on my shelf. Going over, I picked her up. She was so dusty, I hadn't even cleaned her in many months. I used to take care of her everyday, now she was neglected. Cradling her, I lay back on the bed. I stared into her eyes. "Mother, my mother, " I whispered, "help me! I can't do it alone. Oh God, I can't do it alone anymore! I hurt so bad! I want someone to love me, why is that so hard? What have I done? Please, God, help me!" I cried for all the things I had done wrong, as well as everything I attempted out of sheer goodness that had gone unacknowledged.

"I had failed, and Satan was loving every minute of it!

"The Blessed Mother gazed back at me. Was that love I saw in her eyes or was it my imagination? All I knew was that I felt a peace coursing through me.

"God, I needed help!

"The next day I was at a friend's house, she also had the

same statue in her living room. Again, I knelt before her, crying out for her to help me.

"When God closes a door, he opens a window. Just that quick. We spend so much time looking at the closed door, we often don't see that opened window.

"Changing Gaits helped me to see what I was doing that had been so destructive. I needed to take time for me, to hear the wind in the trees, to pray, to listen for God's voice, which had been lost in the thought processes of my head. When was the last time I had done that? In fact, why had I cast Him out of my life at all?

"It was because I wanted to be 'accepted,' and if it meant that God would be on the outside looking in, well, so be it.

"I remembered then. It had been in the innocence of my marriage, when I believed that despite all the pain he inflicted, I could carry on anyway, if only I continued to do everything RIGHT. Then I wouldn't get hurt. It was a comfortable arrangement, because I wasn't rocking the boat, just like when I was growing up at home. "Keep the peace," my dad always told me. I was such a good little girl. I kept the peace.

"I got hurt anyway. Oh well, I tried harder. And harder

still.

> *"Because failure was NOT in my vocabulary!*

> *"But then came the day when my husband told me that he wanted to see me dead and he was the one who could, in his words, "fuckin' do it!" He hurled a cast iron skillet at me. I ducked. It struck the solid oak back door, splitting the skillet in two pieces.*

> *"Had it hit me, I would have died.*

> *"That did it, my 'knight in shining armor' had to go. I couldn't live in that denial phase anymore. I called the police. He was taken away. Then I filed for divorce, moving his things into a new apartment while he was in jail, telling him that he had a new address and to not come home anymore.*

> *"One would think I was happy to finally be free of him. No, I wasn't. Instead, I blamed MYSELF for the failure of that marriage. If only…if only…if only…I thought. If only I had done something better, different. I failed because I wasn't able to "fix" him! I was even told by a Catholic priest that I was responsible for the salvation of **his** soul and, by filing for divorce, I had failed him **and** myself.*

> *"Never mind the fact that I was almost killed, I had failed*

yet again. The priest said so. How could I have doubted him? He was a man of God!

"Despite all the good I had done in my life, I was still going to hell.

"Damn it!

"I gave up on my religion at that point. Hey, if I was going to hell, I might as well live it up!

"I drank!

"I did drugs!

*"I slept with sometimes two or three guys a night, going from one bed to another. I even slept with married men, knowing full well they were cheating on their wives. I gave it **my** blessing as I took the crumbs **they** offered.*

*"I neglected my kids, leaving them at their own mercy for several days at a time while I was out chasing my "dream..." whatever **that** was! I believed all the lies that I had been told by these guys, giving up all of my morals in an all out effort to be "loved." As long as all the liquor they could drink was bought and I lay on my back and performed every sex act they wanted, including many I would never have even conceived of on my own, I could be just what they all wanted me to be...they said they*

"loved" me. In the process, even THEY beat me. I had bruises all over my back, buttocks and hips that looked like I was hit by a truck!

"Then came the night that I innocently went to a man's apartment on the premise of selling his young children my books, that they had wanted to meet 'an author.' My whole world crashed. I was offered cranberry juice over ice. I woke up later to find myself being raped by five black men. My only thought was of survival. "Please, God," I prayed, "let me live through this!"

"I had cheapened myself to a nothing. Less than nothing.

"And Satan smiled back because he knew that he now had me, the once pious and holy lady, in his grasp. I, who had statues of the Blessed Virgin in every room, had now put those statues away where they wouldn't remind me of my failure. All except for the one high up on my bedroom shelf. She still saw me ... and grieved.

"It had seemed soooo long ago, that while I was out walking early one spring morning, I was praying. The eastern sky was tinged with a faint orange glow and my heart was light and happy. In the far distance, I saw a doe, walking placidly along a

fence. I said, "oh, God, if only I could see a deer up close, that would be so neat!" Just then, I heard a faint clop, clop, clop of tiny hooves. Stopping and turning my head ever so slightly, I saw a fawn walking right up to me! I dared to not even breathe!

"The little fawn stepped closer...closer, until she was only inches from me. Despite the gnats that buzzed in my ears and eyes, I didn't blink, I didn't breathe. She wriggled her little nose, staring at me, until she realized that I was a human! AGH! Off she bounded, until she was gone. I was ecstatic! I had seen something very few people witness: a completely wild fawn, trusting enough to stand beside me, if only for a few seconds. I gave thanks to God over and over for this tiny miracle, and as I turned back for home, the sun was just coming up over the eastern horizon.

"What had happened since then was life and it's realities of the brutality that I had put up with for so long- an abusive husband, men who had used me, my mother had passed away, but not before I had the chance to reconcile with her. She survived three more weeks after that, facing her extremely painful death as if she was paying for the pain she had made of her life. I was so disillusioned by the dreams that had been shattered- I had given *up. Why should I care about God, I thought. He let me down. I had married who I **thought** was my knight in shining armor, I had wanted that "happily ever after," and instead his armor was tarnished, almost from the third day of our marriage when he slapped my face hard- only because I had turned up the heat thermostat without his permission! I was now bereft, alone and unloved. My three greatest fears.*

"And it was all my fault, so I had been told.

"What's scary is that I went from an abusive marital relationship, to one that was also abusive, in that he was drinking himself to death. Did I also mention that he was married? I was having an affair with a married alcoholic who kept promising me, when he was drunk, of course, that he would leave his wife and be with me. I waited. I waited some more. When he was sober, it was a whole different story; he couldn't leave her for all he owed her. She had bailed him out of jail so many times, she was long-suffering, she stood by him. What bullshit! He was a liar as much as I was for believing him, all the while lying to myself that he really loved me. Actually, he really loved drinking and would have done anything for that next bottle to appear. He had sold his soul, just as I had sold mine.

"And Satan smiled because he knew he had us both in his grasp. The weak, the vulnerable.

"I then went on to yet another man in which mind control was the code word of the day. It was so very subtle, I didn't even see it at first, yet I also didn't feel "right," my gut instinct was screaming out, to beware! I was, as I said before, walking on eggshells, too afraid to stand up for myself, because I so desperately wanted this one to work out, damn it! I was so afraid of failure! I was so afraid...to lose him! Yet how can you lose something you never had in the first place? The day to day anxiety wore me out, yet it seemed 'comfortable,' because I had lived with that anxiety all my life. I was so used to it. It was my drug of choice. Daily I would call him, almost as soon as he got off work, just to say hi. He was worn out, tired, as I made small talk, reassuring him that yes, I knew he was exhausted, poor thing, and that I cared. After our conversation, even if it ended with him yelling at me for some tiny thing, I would feel exhilarated, why? Because negative attention is better than no attention at all.

"My other behaviors, fear of failure, fear of abandonment, fear of not being loved, all stemmed from my childhood, which

carried over to adulthood, when I was taken advantage of by people who sensed my vulnerability, my naiveté. I was a real mess!

"Then came my salvation... in the guise of a horse. I felt as though I was reborn.

"A week later, as I sat outside next to the pasture, I was just delighting in being in the presence of God. The horses came up to me, one by one. They sensed that all I needed was to just be in this moment. *I softly talked to them, praying. I listened to the sound of silence, feeling the afternoon sun on my face, giving thanks for the strength that I was receiving from the peace. I breathed in...out...in...their strength, their power, yet also the gentleness they exuded. I looked one horse named Diesel in his big blue eyes, as he stood by me the longest, as if my protector. His knowing eyes conveyed that all would be well, I just needed to trust, much as they trusted me in that moment. 'Let go of your pain and let God back into your life, Diane,' they seemed to convey.*

"One of Guy's dogs came bounding up to me in that moment also. Sandy had been abused also earlier in her life, yet she trusted me enough in the very short time she knew me, to know *that I wouldn't hurt her. She sat next to me, wriggling all over as I rubbed all the scratchy places that dogs love to be rubbed, licking my hand as if to encourage me to continue. I smiled at her antics as she then took off to play with another dog, a black Lab named Oreo.*

"I have much to give thanks for. God has always been there. God will always be here. I just need to trust Him."

Guy has his acronyms, I have one of my own:

TRUST in God:

To

Realize

U are

Safe

Today…in God.

Changing Gaits also has a simple philosophy…WE + HOW + GOD = JOY

We can overcome anything

How thru Honesty, Open mindedness and Willingness

GOD Good Orderly Direction

JOY Jesus first, Others second, Yourself third.

06/24/2007

Chapter Six - Other Testimonies of Hope

Humble yourselves before the Lord and He will life you up.

James 4:10

Describe two ways you can improve your conscious contact with GOD (Good Orderly Direction?)

The Mission Statement of Changing Gaits is very simple, yet very powerful:

"To use the healing bond with horses to teach, guide and encourage positive attitudes and behaviors."

Nothing is so strong as the words and experiences of

others. It is through their pain and wisdom that we ourselves grow.

"Shane is my beautiful, lost 10-year-old. On the outside and most of the time at school and in his studies, Shane appears perfect. It's when he is asked to comply with the rules of the world or to make an appropriate choice that he can't. Shane has always been challenging his "official diagnosis" of ADHD/ODD/SED---a lot of letters for one little boy! Often Shane is withdrawn, empty, it seems nothing matters to him, but that is the tuff guy surface; he tries so hard to deal with the everyday demands of life that after awhile he just explodes with so much anger and rage. He has few friends and is very much the outsider.

"My family's experience at Changing Gaits started in June 2007 with six words, "Mommy, maybe that would help me." Those words from a child with (five) years of therapy who never voices a need for help, stopped me in my tracks. All I heard from the TV was, "For more information, go to the WCCO Web site....." I went to bed that night knowing that no matter what it took, I was going to see if "something with horses" could reach a child that has been unreachable for years, and growing more violent and angry. The next day I clicked on the web site to Changing

*Gaits and a new relationship with my son and our family. Within a week, Shane and I were at the ranch with an amazing man, Guy Kaufman, and this amazing idea about equine therapy and kids. I knew in the first hour we were there that we had FINALLY found someplace that had the possibility of a breakthrough and give my son and society some hope in and for his life. He went from all of his issues, to "maybe that would help me," to a child that is using his coping skills, taking in what he is learning and using it. It's not perfect, but it's more progress then I have seen. Since starting Changing Gaits, we have had only one issue where we had to call the crisis team; he no longer destroys his room, he is much more respectful, and he has a confidence about him that I have never seen. The difference is day and night. Changing Gaits is a very committed program and you have to put in a lot of effort as a family, but it all pays off." *-Jessica

The obstacle course, which is set up in the arena, represents our hurdles in life, which can be a hodgepodge of miasma that can drag us down. The horse is lead by the person who is using it as a metaphor for the issues that confront her/him. There are also distractions for the horses such as hay, which represent our temptations. Just when you think you have the horse controlled, meaning controlling the issue or issues that bogs you down, the horse decides to want that hay so bad. Then the retort comes, *"are you going to let your addict feed on that stuff, or are you going to pull him away?"*

Frustrations well up as the lead rope is yanked, the horse goes his way and the person the other. The person needs to work in tandem *with* the addiction, as opposed to letting the addiction control *him or her*. A strategy is needed. It is OK to remove those obstacles, as opposed to having to work and maneuver around them.

"In recovery, you have to create a strategy for getting your addict through an obstacle course, even if it means going ahead, identifying the challenges and removing the ones you are able to," Guy said. *"We grow when we are uncomfortable. It is important to remember we always have choices. Insight gleaned from one session with a horse is as beneficial as ten in the therapists chair."*

Katie's testimony:

"Guy, how can I put this? You have taught me a lot, that I can trust people again, how to trust and how to trust God. You have shown me what path I should take, and I have chosen to walk it. You know that I am almost 17 years old and I love you as a dad I have never had.

"My faith is getting stronger every day and I have you to thank. I'm not forgetting about Cheryl, she is another person I can thank for the changes in my life. I thank you guys a lot for all the effort and love that you have shown me. Now I can show the same love and effort to other people. I'm ready to change my life, get off the road that I'm on and onto the Lord's path of rightness. My mom and me are getting along better. I thank you guys so much for showing me the way of the Lord."

Brittany's letter:

"Dear Guy,

Thank you for showing me how to reign in my problems. You use a very wonderful technique. Maggie May was very patient with us. After everything that happened to me, my dad does not deserve a second chance. But we don't deserve a second chance either, yet God gave us a second chance. You have a wonderful ministry there.

Thanks for everything, -Brittany"

"Thank you, Changing Gaits, your patience, guidance and exposure to Good, Orderly Direction gave my group a belief in the possibility of change. In the disguise of a horse, you offered them something they rarely touch in their daily lives, HOPE. You have planted invaluable seeds. I look forward to a successful connection."

Other letters of testimony from teens all have the same theme: TRUST. *"You have taught me that I can trust people again. That I can trust God."* Another says, *"I hope that you're proud of the changes I have made."* (Self esteem = Approval.) Still another, *"Now I can show love."* (Acceptance.)

Even Guy himself says, *"Shadow is all about experience, strength and hope. He has been that horse I can look to when I think about quitting. Faith tells us to keep going, to keep plugging away. I continue to believe this is God's call and that we are going to make a difference in this insurmountable field of addiction that seems to be running rampant in society."*

Steve's story:

Steve has been through chemical dependency treatment eight times and is now sober. At first, he didn't appear comfortable around the horse, Dozer, as he took the lead rope for his first exercise, the obstacle course. It was there that Steve learned that he and the horse had a few things in common. Dozer balked when Steve tried to lead him away from the hay through the course, prompting Steve to remark, "that's a lot like me!" His struggle with Dozer to make him go where he wanted was a metaphor that Steve realized mirrored his own life. When he was finished, Guy had Steve do it again, this time blindfolded. Guy had moved some obstacles, showing that we can make the same mistakes under different circumstances.

"What do you do when obstacles," meaning obstacles to your recovery, *"get in the way?"* Guy asked him.

"Oh, I walk around them," Steve said. In a moment of

epiphany, he added, *"if I don't move then out of my way, they'll just be there when I come through again!"*

"Steve, ya gotta kick them out of your way!" Guy said, knocking aside a hurdle for emphasis.

One swift kick was for the casinos that Steve frequented, another kick was for using friends and the way was now clear, both in the arena and in obstacles to Steve's recovery.

"This really works," said Steve, as he ended the day's program. *"I've been through treatment eight times, but I've never had it explained this clearly."* The spiritual component of the program has also been a big factor in his new sobriety, something other programs were lacking.

Shane's story:

Shane, a cowboy from Texas, went through seven treatment programs, plus spent time in jail for a DWI, came to Changing Gaits and within days of interaction with the horses, something clicked within him, changing his life. He realized that his problems weren't all about drugs and alcohol, but rather, the way he dealt with life. He mentioned how Guy and Shadow were there to guide him through a gauntlet of emotions with understanding, patience and love. *"Unlike with people,"* he says, *"you can't manipulate a horse, therefore you are forced to deal with your problems."* Shane got sober before moving back to Texas, hoping to open a similar facility there.

"Lord, tell me your ways, show me how to live Guide me in Your truth and teach me, my God and Savior. I trust you all day long." -Psalm 25:4

Chapter Seven - Future Stories of Hope?

HOW (Honesty, Open mindedness and Willingness) has your past behavior been outside your value system?

"If we confess our sins, he is faithful and just and will forgive us our sins and purify us from all unrighteousness." 1 John 1:9

Sammy's story:

    "*Sammy never knew his father. His mother was a prostitute all her life. Sammy was sexually abused many times over by the 'tricks' she had brought home. She also had two extremely abusive marriages, in which she was beaten daily. It was in between these marriages that she turned back to "hookin'," as Sammy had* *called it.*

"At age thirteen, Sammy began drinking to medicate himself from the pain. By the time he was sixteen, he was also dealing in drugs, as well as ingesting anything and everything he could get his hands on.

"His mother suffered a brain aneurysm, rendering her to spending the next fourteen years in a nursing home until she died, unable to care for herself. At this point, Sammy lived on the streets, basically fending for himself. He dropped out of school, dealing in drugs, fighting to survive, becoming a male prostitute himself. The drinking continued. By the time I met him, he was 42 years old, with seven DWI's under his belt. He had literally spent a third of his life in jails, and went through treatment twice- and failed, because he went through the motions merely to satisfy the needs of the state. He was bitter, angry and resentful of the fact that his mom, whom he considered his best friend, was taken from him way too soon.

"Raised a Catholic, he became agnostic, feeling that God had abandoned him at some point, so why bother with that stuff. He went through the motions of his treatments without giving them a second chance. When asked by his treatment counselor who his

Higher Power was, Sammy's reply was that the only person he believed in was himself. Considered a felon, he couldn't even get hired to pump gas. Depression became his friend. He told me that sleep was elusive, because he feared for the demons inside his head that taunted him on a near constant basis. He drank so heavily, more than anyone I have ever known. After an eighteen pack, he could still speak, slurring his words only a little.

*"I was Sammy's codependent. I loved him deeply. I tried to "save him, to change him," yet I also enabled him. I wanted his love and approval **so bad,** that I bought him the booze he needed to stay alive. Yes, you read that right. Sammy was so addicted to alcohol, that without it, he would have died, just as with it he would have died. He needed it. I was afraid he'd get yet another DWI, which would mean prison time for him, so I went to the liquor store myself for him. The alternative was that he would sneak money from my purse and take the keys to my car and go himself.*

"When Sammy was drunk, he told me everything that I wanted to hear, all the words of praise that I yearned for. It was as much of an addiction/obsession for me to hear those words in my love starved mind as much as it was for him to drink. We

were two of a kind. Soul mates who could laugh together and cry together as well.

"Unfortunately, he was married; I had been cheating with him on his wife. I was waiting for him to leave her so that we could live in that happily ever after that I had envisioned. When he was drunk, he would tell me that yes, today was THE day, he was finally leaving her for me. He even came to my place for several days at a time. I was in heaven. I began to realize, however, that when he began to sober up, the regrets began, he would make excuses to me about needing to get back to her. I was incensed. 'What about me' I cried out.

"Don't make this harder on us than it is!" he replied. "You had me for a few days. Now I owe it to her to go back."

"Thus continued a cycle of abuse that I had brought upon myself. What the hell, I deserved it, right? After all, I was responsible for the breakup of my marriage. My kids were floundering in some haze of confusion and loss. None of that mattered to me, because I myself was floundering.

"And no one cared.

"Sadly, it was Sammy's addiction that finally caught up with him. His probation officer caught him drinking when she

made an unannounced visit to his house. By six p.m., he had gone through an 18 pack of beer and a fifth of pure vodka, which he drank straight from the bottle as if it were nothing more than water. I was horrified when I saw that nearly empty bottle in his cooler, I knew deep in my gut that something bad would happen. Immediately, he was arrested and was sentenced to serve two years in prison. He cast me out of his life, telling me to "fuck off," and that I was the cause of his addiction because I had supplied him with liquor. Partly true, but on the day he was arrested, he had bought his own booze. In his denial, I think he forgot that I had only known him for two years, yet he had been drinking for thirty.

"Addiction does that to people. Irresponsible, they blame others instead of themselves, just like I did. Ironically, Sammy has a friend named Brad. Brad is also a many time drinking offender. I also did many favors for Brad, to gain his approval as well. Finally, I had had enough. As Guy said in reference to himself, I became sick and tired of being sick and tired of being their "savior" only when they needed to be bailed out of the trouble they themselves got into.

"It is my hope that when he is released from prison, that

Sammy will come to Changing Gaits, to heal. Because, although he is dry in prison, once he is in the free world again, he will be too tempted to stay sober. It is too ingrained in him. To be able to do that, though, he needs to let go of his belief in himself and allow God to come into his life and be that Higher Power of good."

Paul's story:

"Paul is a friend I have known for two years. A big bear of a man, his gentle heart is so filled with pain, which has manifested itself through his addictions to cocaine and alcohol.

"Paul is the youngest of four kids, all raised in a proper, Catholic home. He was always considered by his father to be the black sheep of the family, no matter how hard he tried, he couldn't break that belief. At age 42, the pain of that belief drove him to attempt suicide. While recovering in the hospital, he cried, "God, why am I still alive? I don't want to live!"

"Paul could not see a purpose in his life, he was merely existing. And so, he became addicted to cocaine and alcohol to cover the pain. He could not hold down a full time job; usually

within days or weeks, he either quit or was fired. He had two marriages, both broke up due to his addictions. The loss of his second marriage merely added to his crumbling self esteem. 'This gal,' he said to me, 'was his soul mate, yet in her eyes,' he could do nothing right.

"He went through a treatment program offered through the Veteran's hospital, dealing with the demons that was his life. Months after his discharge, he still found it difficult to hold down a job, so he lived with his elderly parents due to a lack of income, which meant that he had to listen to his father's daily taunts about what a loser he was. He mourned the loss of his marriage; his father's constant diatribes also wore him out. Many times, Paul verbalized that he wished he had successfully committed suicide, that at this point, he was only going through the motions of life.

*"I could only sit and listen as he told me this story. This was after my epiphany at Changing Gaits. Miracle of miracles, for me, I had NO desire to "fix" his life, other than to hold his hand, pray for him and offer to just be a friend. Incredibly, I also had **no** desire to want to supply him with booze when he asked me to, instead, I told him I couldn't stand by and watch him destroy himself.*

"Why not?" he demanded. "I have already fucked it up, might as well go all the way and prove everybody right!"

"I had no desire to offer platitudes to that remark. It wasn't that I didn't care, because I did. I have known Paul long enough to see his good side. But I also see the good side of me now, and I am not going to let another man pull me down with him any longer.

Paul would also be a perfect candidate for Changing Gaits, much as Sammy would. They both have a compassion for animals that would allow them to work with the horses. However, they have to WANT to be healed.

How low do you have to go before you finally admit that you need help?

Probably as low as I did, that you feel so weak, like you are slogging through wet cement, unable to move forward anymore. It's when you become uncomfortable with your life that you either sink…or choose to swim.

I choose to save myself.

Chris's story:

"*Chris comes from a Catholic family of seven siblings. He spent the first twelve years of his life in Paynesville, MN before moving to Grantsburg, WI. The reason for the move was because his mother was tired of the emotional abuse her alcoholic husband was heaping on the entire family. Chris's oldest sister lived in Grantsburg, so, like thieves in the night, mom packed up the kids. They literally left everything behind in their flight to be free of the devastating pain.*

"*Starting over for Chris was not easy when one is twelve, just entering puberty. He ruled Grantsburg, getting into his fair share of trouble. He became known as the family's black sheep. He married a gal right out of high school because she was pregnant with their first child. That marriage produced three children in seven years before it crumbled under the weight of her affair with his best friend. He then took up with another gal. That relationship was rocky for nine years and he walked away from it. After a year, she contacted him and he returned. She promised it would be better, so they married.*

"It only became worse, but by now, there were two more children involved, so he stuck it out, for their sake.

"Although Chris never became an alcoholic like his father, he hid behind drugs and in being the tough guy. He told me once of an incident when he pulled his best friend's body out of the St Croix River after a weekend boating accident.

"I rarely cry," he had said, "but that was one of the few times I did."

"He often referred to his father as, "the rotten bastard." He never had the chance at reconciliation with him before his death. Chris lives in isolation and has few friends, with the exception of his children, he rarely went anywhere or did anything. He kept his feelings bottled up, developing a sense of independence. "I can do it all by myself, I don't need anyone doing it for me! I have bailed myself out when I was in jail, I didn't ask for anyone's help!" And in anger to me, he railed, "I don't need for YOU to buy

my love either!" Yet he went way overboard to buy his kids' love, anything they wanted, he bought it, or did it. He bragged how they "loved" him more than their mothers. When I met with his two youngest children, to me, they seemed very spoiled; always begging until he caved in and gave them whatever they wanted.

"He had a fear of going to church alone, so he stopped, instead criticizing the ones who did attend, calling them hypocrites, including his ex-wife, who took his children there every Sunday. He didn't like walking into any situation in which he didn't know anyone. He isolated himself from all scrutiny, so as to not be judged. He had tattoos running up and down his arms, long hair, a "rock star" image that he hid behind. He was trying to be something he wasn't because he didn't like himself at all.

"The one time I cried in front to him, he said that if I ever did that again, we were through. I couldn't express anger either, because that just set him off. I couldn't be "me." I had resorted to walking on eggshells, or, as I called it, "eggs-hell," because I no longer could trust when he'd go off and berate me, much like his father must have berated him.

"The second week I went to his house, he proudly showed

me three books that he had on his book shelf. Immediately, I felt a chill run through me, though I didn't know why. An uneasiness assailed me, I felt evil in that room.

"These are the three books of Satan," he said, rubbing the covers. "I feel honored to have them."

"I raised my eyebrows, wondering why he would feel the need to have these books. Looking at him, I said, 'they are evil! Why do you feel you need those? If you believe in God as you say you do, you don't need this.' Quickly, I looked to the crucifix that he had on the wall by my head, trying to take comfort in that, the sign under it asked, "Got God?"

"Instead, he explained, 'Why do I need to close myself off from knowing both sides? I know the Bible, why can't I also know about this? It is my intent before I die, to read these.' He put them back on the shelf.

*"I should have run as fast as I could from him at that point, and not looked back. But it was my desire- **my obsession!** to have his approval; once more, I felt I could work through that, too. But then it began to dawn on me, his penchant for always wearing black, his love of the music on a well known radio station that always spoke of death, suicide, of getting even when people*

hurt you. He once told his sister that his heart would always be black. He wore on a chain, both a skull as well as a cross. He had tattoos on his body, one of a devil woman, and many others , proclaiming his lust for the "other side." He wore his hair long.

"Oh, God, I should have run! He reveled in the sins of lust, pride, greed, envy, rage. Looking back on it now, no wonder he couldn't love me, that is not an emotion the devil has.

"And I was running with the devil. Satan had seduced me. He won, pure and simple. What's interesting was that eight years before, when my then-husband had an affair, I prayed for Jesus to help me. One night, I felt a huge weight on my chest. I couldn't move. I was paralyzed. I smelled hot sulfur and felt a huge hand literally rip my heart out. A demonic laugh ensued and the devil proclaimed that he wanted me to give up my soul. Three times I rebuked him in Jesus' name. Three times, he screamed fiercely at me, 'God DAMN you, you bitch!' I was so scared! I tried to wake my husband up, I said, 'Help me, I'm being possessed by the devil!'

"He slept on. The last time, I saw my mother's visage behind the devil as he laughed and said, 'I'll be back for you!' Then he left. My heart was beating so fast, I grabbed my Pieta

statue, *saying Our father and Hail Mary over and over and over....then put it in the back of my head. Sure enough, he came back again, not viciously, but rather, with the smooth seduction of one who knows how to tempt...and win.*

"Sadly, it was all the latent ideas of his that gradually pushed Chris away from me. Those three books of Satan. His refusal to share of himself, his fear of losing control over his life, his fear of loving someone else in the event of being hurt, all combined to create within him the walls that he built so high to keep others out. Right from the start, he told me that trust didn't come easy to him. I asked him 'do you trust me?'

"His reply, 'only until you give me a reason not to.'

"My mistake came when I told him, only two weeks into our relationship, that I loved him, saying it during a grateful moment- out of friendship. It scared him to no end. I followed it up with a very sincere letter, which he said was the most beautiful letter that anyone had ever sent to him, but that scared him as well. That was when he brought out the bricks and mortar, withdrawing deep inside himself.

"He didn't feel worthy because his father made sure to cut him down at every turn. Emotional abuse is harder than physical

abuse to overcome, because words wielded so powerfully can hurt so much more and leave a lasting impact longer than bruises can. Feeling emotionally worthless, Chris' vulnerability allowed Satan the 'in' that he needed. Chris has a gentle, but extremely troubled soul, that he hid behind with drugs. To want to be in control, to have the last say in his relationship, to call the shots, to dictate when he can and can't feel love, these are all his armors of defense that I couldn't seem to break through. I had thought that I could change him, to "fix" it, to kiss the hurts and make it better. Like with Paul, like with Sammy, I can no longer take the responsibility for the troubles in their lives. I can listen, I can provide support, but I cannot change their ways of thinking. That is between them and God."

"I know that God promises to never give me any more than I can handle. I just wish He didn't trust me so much!" - Mother Teresa

"Therefore, confess your sins to each other and pray for each other so that you may be healed. The prayer of a righteous man is powerful and effective." -James 5:16

Chapter Eight - What is Changing Gaits About?

"Do unto others as you would have them do unto you."

-Luke 6:31

Who do you need to make amends to and HOW (Honesty, Open mindedness and Willingness) will you do that?

A testimony from Bar None Residential Treatment Center:

    "Changing Gaits has truly impacted the Sunrise Unit in many ways. Residents enjoy going to Changing Gaits to learn about themselves and what it is like to work together as a team. Changing Gaits has increased self-esteem in many residents and given them the courage and strength to move forward in their

Diane Ganzer

lives. *The residents truly benefit from the program. Some of their comments include, 'I learned to work on treatment' 'I learned to look at myself for things I am doing' 'Learned how to ask for help' 'It makes you feel better about yourself by talking about your feelings to other people....it makes me feel better about myself'."*
-Judy Mork

This next letter is written here exactly how it was received by a young participant:

"I was walk with a horse when the night comes. He showed me how two ride a horse. With the staff I hook up with the horse. They give me a come place in my heart. You give me a horse that give me a spacil thing. You give me the one thing you give me is two love the horse that you give me is Shadow is the one that will stand for love me. I will stand by Shadow for a long time. I want Shadow to stand by my side. If I have to work with a new horse then I will give my heart. If I work with a deferent horse then I have to give my love to the horse like Shadow."

It is so obvious that Shadow knows exactly why he is needed here, he is doing God's work just as much as Guy is! The feeling of love and peace in this child's heart is so evident!

This next original letter was sent to Guy from a boy who attended Changing Gaits. It has been left in it's entirety so that you can see for yourself the wisdom gleaned from what happens when one is changed by just being in the peace and serenity of God.

Diane Ganzer

Dear Guy ▓▓▓▓▓▓ thank you for the
horse rides and for giving me some
time to get to know more and I'm still
haveing promblem and dont know what
to do or how to get it out of the
way I need some one like you to teak
to Because I tryed talking to everybody
here and they keep telling me the same
thing that I'm a better kid then what
I act like and I know I am
an I need to do why I'm here
is to trust the people that put the
rag ▓▓▓▓ over my eyes and I
know that if I dont get all of the
help that I need here I know that
the man in the sky can give me an
the help that I need

I will Be looking foward to
seeing you agian

            If I cant see you
I can always see the person I
was when I was out their and
I can still see skooter ha ha

78

This next letter, I must warn you, is heart wrenching, but true. Written by a young participant, it makes one give thanks to God for the saving grace of Changing Gaits, reaffirming why it is present…there but for the grace of God, goes this child.

"When I was born, I could have died. I was abused when I was seven. I have run from people for a long time. When I trust people, it is going to take time. I was in DC where I was raised. I have fought with people, I have been beaten with a belt. I have been thrown to the floor and kicked on the ground…I have tried to hurt myself; I have taken batteries and eaten the stuff out of it. I have scars on my hand fgor picking on myself. I had windows broke on me, I have broke windows with my hand. I have been turned to the wrong thing.

"I will put my faith and the love that I have told my God he will protect me in my path. I will give my life to the Lord. If it is your will to protect me, I will follow You. I know you have lead me in Your path. I know that with me working with the horses that I will learn to trust things and people. I will put my trust in the Lord, he protects me from evil. Lord, see me in the midst where you are." -Jason

This testimonial speaks about the "tough-guy" pride that fell by the wayside, all because of what the horses meant to them:

"I am a juvenile probation supervisor and work with Juvenile Substance Abuse Court in Ramsey County. We started having our clients attend Changing Gaits several weeks ago. All of our clients have significant drug/alcohol abuse issues. They range in age from 15-17, and many have significant criminal histories. Right now, all of our participants are boys. We have made two trips so far, with four more to come.

"The first group was interesting, because the guys were nervous and reluctant to participate, and I really didn't know what to expect. After an overview of the program and safety, they were told to get their tools-halter and lead rope- and go catch a horse. It was both amusing and touching to watch these tough guys try to accomplish this task. They all did it, all in their own ways, mastering their own fears. During the process, the staff were encouraging them. Then, the young men walked back to the barn with their horses, all a little prouder, more confident and having learned something about themselves.

"The program has an immediate impact on the participants,

and on observers as well. It is a powerful way to help people see how their emotions and behaviors impact their lives. I'm excited we've had the opportunity to participate in Changing Gaits."

- Mary Pat Dunlap

So what is Changing Gaits all about? For starters...

Changing Gaits follows the premises of the Twelve Steps. Without having God in our lives, we are powerless to change ourselves. Below are the Twelve Steps.

1. I admitted that I am powerless over my circumstances and that my life had become unmanageable.

2. I have accepted that God, through the power of the Holy Spirit, in Jesus' name, can restore my sanity, redeem my circumstances, repair my relationships, heal my wounds and set me free from all evil and self and worldly domination.

3. I have accepted Jesus Christ as my Lord and Savior and have committed my will, my loved ones and all things pertaining to my life to the care and control of God (as He knows Himself to be) and have asked for and received the baptism of the holy Spirit.

4. I have asked God the Father, in Jesus' name that the

holy spirit would reveal to me the truth about myself.

5. I have admitted to God and to myself and to another human being the exact nature of my wrongs and have received forgiveness through the Blood of Jesus who cleanses us from all sin and unrighteousness. Have purposed to forgive myse;lf and to forget my past sins, to instead press on to the high calling in Chris Jesus.

6. Have prepared myself through the diligent study of the Word of God and have asked God, in Jesus' name to remove all known sin in my life as I stand on the promises in the Word for redemption and restoration.

7. Have humbly come before the Throne of Grace and have asked the Lord to keep me from evil and to form Chris in me, in Jesus' name.

8. Have asked the Holy Spirit to show me by the Word of God, where, when, how and whom I have offended and have been willing to make amends to these individuals and am eager for reconciliation.

9. Made direct amends by asking forgiveness to such peole (whenever possible) as led by the Holy Spirit only.

10. Continue each day to acknowledge and confess all

sin as the Holy Spirit convicts me and to receive forgiveness through the Blood of Jesus. Continue to remain willing to assume responsibility for my actions and when convicted, promptly admit it.

11. Seek, through prayer the Word of God to improve my relationship with God, praying for knowledge of His will for my life and for the Power of the Holy Spirit to carry that out, in Jesus' name.

12. After having accepted Jesus Christ, I have tried to carry the Gospel message and my testimony to others. I have purposed to live these twelve principles in all my life's affairs in Jesus' Name.

It is only when we are *"sick and tired of being sick and tired"* of our addictions and behaviors that our lives will change. Becoming uncomfortable with the daily hell that we face, unable to put one foot even in front of the other anymore, much like slogging through wet cement, is when we desire change. The tools that Changing Gaits has, horse therapy, faith in God and the belief that you can be healed, are all steps in the direction of healing.

EAAS is an emerging field in which horses are used to

assist for emotional growth and learning to address issues related to substance abuse, along with problems in communication, relationships, and behavior. It is a collaborative effort between a licensed therapist and a horse specialist who work together to design sessions that require the client to apply certain skills while participating in activities with the horse.

EAAS is not riding or horsemanship; in fact, 90% of the activities with the horse take place on the ground, and require the participant to apply certain skills, i.e., non-verbal communication, creative thinking, and problem solving the rough processing feelings, behaviors, and patterns. This form of therapy has been proven to bring faster results than traditional treatment/counseling alone, as the participants learn very quickly about themselves and are able to relate the exercises they perform with the horses to real-life situations.

EAAS is based on EAGALA techniques, and is effective for all ages (Children, Teenagers, Adults, Families, Groups).

Examples of Activities Performed:

Temptation Alley Obstacle Course: Involves leading a horse through an alley with the hay on one side and grain on the other side, without letting the horse eat any of it!   This activity is done without touching the horse. This helps determine the obstacles in our lives that keep us from being emotionally healthy.

Life's Little Obstacles: Leading a horse over a jump without touching or talking to it. Used to learn new ways of non-verbal communication.

These are just two of the two-hundred plus activities available.

The author and Sandy on a trail ride!

For Those Who've Been There Before, We Humbly Acknowledge....

How (Honesty, Open mindedness and Willingness) will you embrace the lessons learned today for a different tomorrow?

"Therefore, if you are offering your gift at the altar and there remember that your brother has something against you, leave your gift there in front of the altar. First go and be reconciled to your brother; then come and offer your gift."

-Matthew 5:23-24

Rock star Nikki Sixx of Motley Crue fame nearly died from a heroin overdose in 1987. Since his recovery, he has been working with at risk kids through Covenant House. The next song detail his feelings after his near death experience, when his heart actually stopped, which sums up what most people going through addiction issues of any sort deal with- that they have to hit bottom before they can come back up.

Life Is Beautiful

You can't quit until you try,
You can't live until you die,
You can't learn to tell the truth,
Until you learn to lie.

You can't breathe until you choke.
You gotta laugh when you're the joke,
There's nothing like a funeral to make you feel alive.

Just open your eyes
Just open your eyes
And see that life is beautiful.
Will you swear on your life,
That no one will cry at my funeral?

I know some things that you don't,
I've done things that you won't,
There's nothing like a trail of blood
to find your way back home .

I was waiting for my hearse,
What came next was so much worse,
It took a funeral to make me feel alive!

Just open your eyes
Just open your eyes
And see that life is beautiful.
Will you swear on your life,
That no one will cry at my funeral?

Just open your eyes
Just open your eyes
And see that life is beautiful.
Will you swear on your life,
That no one will cry at my funeral?

Just open your eyes

Just open your eyes
And see that life is beautiful.
Will you swear on your life,
That no one will cry at my funeral?

Just open your eyes
Just open your eyes
And see that life is beautiful.
Will you swear on your life,
That no one will cry at my funeral?

<u>"Life is Beautiful"</u> Lyrics courtesy Sixx A.M. *The Heroin Diaries* soundtrack.

This next one expresses a wish for second chances, which is what everyone going through addictions realizes that they ARE capable of, a second chance! They only need the opportunity to be given it! Changing Gaits is all about that! Sometimes, it is saying goodbye to an addiction, being given that "second chance" at life to prove what they really are capable of!

Second Chance

My eyes are open wide

By the way, I made it through the day,

I watched the world outside,

By the way, I'm leaving out today

I just saw Haley's Comet, she waved,

Said "why you always running in place?

Even the man in the Moon disappears

somewhere in the Stratosphere."

Tell my mother,

tell my father,

I've done the best I can.

To make them realize

This is my life.

I hope they understand.

I'm not angry,

I'm just saying

Sometimes goodbye

is a second chance.

Please don't cry one tear for me,

I'm not afraid of what I have to say.

This is my one and only voice,

So listen close, it's only for today.

I just saw Haley's Comet, she waved,

Said "why you always running in place?

Even the man in the Moon disappears

somewhere in the Stratosphere"

Tell my mother,

tell my father

I've done the best I can.

To make them realize

This is my life.

I hope they understand.

I'm not angry,

I'm just saying,

Sometimes goodbye

is a second chance .

Here is my chance.

This is my chance.

Tell my mother,

tell my father,

I've done the best I can

To make them realize

This is my life.

I hope they understand.

I'm not angry,

I'm just saying

Sometimes goodbye

is a second chance

Sometimes goodbye

Is a second chance .

"Second Chance" lyrics by: Shinedown

Prayer tree

Aftermath

Who and what strengthens you?

"So, if you think that you are standing firm, be careful that you don't fall."

- 1 Corinthians 10:12

It was a beautiful early November day when I pulled into the driveway to Changing Gaits. I welcomed it like an old friend, as I surveyed the horses out in the pasture, the soft wind caressing my face. I had brought my seventeen year old daughter, Theresa, and her best friend since preschool, Sandy, to partake in this fine day of nothing but horseback riding, at Guy's invitation.

Theresa had been affected by the divorce also, only because she had witnessed the emotional pain that I thought I had hidden so well. She had her own thoughts about her father and I did nothing to change them. I also did nothing to add to them either; she is a big girl and can make up her own mind about what she has experienced.

Guy greeted us warmly, then saddled up four horses. After giving the girls a demonstration of what to expect, we set out.

The trails were soggy from recent rains and the horses carefully picked their way through the mud and slop. I was deep in thought and prayer, when it suddenly hit me.

My epiphany.

The mud represented all the dreck that I had been dealing with over the years. I had been feeling defeated, as if nothing in my life would ever come together. Then, it was almost as if God read my thoughts, and He intervened.

"Diane, do you see that mud down there and how the horse is plodding along, sometimes becoming resistant to your commands? She has a mind of her own and you need to steer her, controlling her just like you need to control your own addictive behavior."

"*Yes, Lord,*" I thought.

"Yet, it is no longer you that is going through that mud, it is now Me. I am carrying you, just as the horse is now carrying you. I have you on my back, you have been lifted up. Let me carry you. Take my yoke, for my load is easy and the burden light."

It reminded me then of the "Footprints" poem, 'it was then that God carried me.'

Yes, I wasn't in this alone. God was there.

"Can we go to the Prayer Tree?" I asked Guy.

"Yes, we'll circle around this trail, then we'll be there," he replied.

Once there, he said a beautiful prayer, full of warmth and gratitude for everything the Lord had given him in this day. I was moved by the Holy Spirit, so I also offered my own prayer of thanksgiving. I felt lifted up, lighter than I had in quite awhile.

All the way home, Theresa had nothing but good things to say about Changing Gaits. She was very impressed with the peace and serenity that it offers and, on her own, with no prompting from me, responded, *"You know, after one afternoon there, I feel as though I had several sessions with a counselor."*

She went back to staring out the car window as the scenery sped by, but I was amazed! I have read the testimonials, I knew what others had been saying, and now she also felt the ministry that Changing Gaits is all about.

I can't say it was easy for me after that either; much like what Guy initially experienced, it is the tiny little steps that we take each day that add up to a lot. I was still affected by the breakup of my last relationship... Even though Chris was stubborn and full of the pride that destroyed the happiness I had originally felt early on in the relationship, I mourned the loss of what "could have been," as well as what was- namely, the fact that I couldn't "fix" him, change him, make him see just how beautiful life really could be. Some days the tears just flowed and I felt that once again, I was sinking into an abyss, unable to climb out. The old feelings of not being worthy of anyone crept in, those feelings of loss, abandonment, insecurity that would keep me awake at night.

I could hear the taunts of Satan, "you're not worthy of anyone, you'll never find anyone, you're a failure..." It was then that I held my medal of Our Lady of Perpetual Help in my clasped hand, praying, begging God to take away those demonic thoughts.

I pulled out the journal Guy had given me. Reading through the list of things listed, one caught my eye.

"I now make a list of all the persons I have harmed in thought, word or deed and a list of all persons I believe have harmed me and I will make amends to all of them."

Amends. Forgiveness. Reconciliation.

Taking out a sheet of paper, I began writing a letter to Chris. In it, I thanked him for what we did have, that I have many bittersweet memories. I wished him good luck in his future and that I let him go with love. Sealing it in an envelope, I walked to the mailbox, giving the letter a kiss before I dropped it in. Whether or not he forgave me was not the issue, I did what *I* had to do.

I followed it up with a phone call the next day. When he answered, I said, "Chris, it's Diane. You don't have to talk, just listen."

The line went dead. He had hung up on me.

I sat, staring at the phone for five minutes.

Ten minutes.

I was numb with grief.

The next day, I got a call from my publisher. Chris had asked to have his name taken off of a book we did together. He wanted to put as much distance between me and him as possible, my publisher said. Again, I felt the anger rise up. I wanted to get even. Take his name off? NO! It would stay! I would hold him to it and he could take me to court if he wished. I no longer cared. It was all about pride. MY pride!

Was I any different from him at that point?

Pride? Lust? Greed?

Instead, I pulled out the journal once more.

"I now go directly to these persons to forgive and to seek forgiveness, restitution or release, whenever and with whomever possible, unless to do so would cause further hurt."

"Oh, God, this is so hard! Why do I always have to be the one to give in...?" I thought. Tears poured down my face as I wept.

Taking a huge breath, I dialed his number once more. When he answered, I prayed he wouldn't hang up.

"Hello?" he answered.

It was so good to hear his voice, even that one word!

Sadly, I began: *"Chris, you win. Go ahead, take your name off that book, if it makes you feel better. I won't fight you on this, I want us to go on to new beginnings. It's OK, go ahead. Thanks."* I then hung up, not waiting for his response, the lump in my throat threatened to suffocate me even as my heart hammered away so fast in my chest, I thought it would fly out of it's own accord.

I couldn't have felt that forgiveness if not for...Changing Gaits.

Yes, I was changing my own gait in midstep, and doing a good job of it, too.

"I now consciously and prayerfully continue to "walk in the light," by unceasingly taking personal inventory of all my temptations and sins and by keeping a constantly open relationship with God, myself and other persons."

"Let the Word of Christ dwell in you richly as you teach and admonish one another with all wisdom, and as you sing psalms, hymns and spiritual songs with gratitude in your hearts to God." - Colossians 3:16

"God said:

"You have read so much. You have heard so much. You have studied. You have sought. You seek still. You know so much, and you know that you are supposed to be happy, and yet happiness eludes you. Rather, happiness weaves in and out of your life.

"There are times when you have thought that happiness was yours, and then, unbeknownst to you, happiness slipped away. You were not looking. Your happiness becomes like a baby

princess who has been stolen away and replaced with a distorted changeling. Without your knowing how or when, it is like a piece of coal was left in the place of the joyful baby princess you once held.

"Discouragement and despair enter. Your heart is turned into that piece of coal. It is unimaginable how the princess of happiness could be so easily replaced and the queen of love shot out the window of your heart and blown into smithereens.

"You know better, and yet, the moment seems to come when despair is your partner, buys you out, takes over and becomes the rule of the day. Something has come upon you. One moment you were King/Queen of the Castle, and now you're not. You wander the terrain of your life, and you wonder where is happiness? Where did it go? When will it come back? Will it ever come back?

"Suddenly you have become bitter and inconsolable. Emptiness assaults your heart, where your heart once was. What do you do now?

"Here's what to do, beloveds. Consider this desolation like a dance that you sit out. Despair has come up to you and asked you to dance.

"You say, "No, thank you. I'll sit out this dance. I will notice you on the dance floor, but I am not going to have you put your arms around me, and I am not going to dance with you. I am not going to join you. ___**I don't have to join you**___. I will not have you lead me. Soon this dance will be over, and I will return to my heart, or my heart will return to me. In any case, you will leave. You have tried to insert yourself into my life. You have accosted me. You have stuck your foot in the door, and, yet**, you do not have the key to my heart and my life.** You might as well leave now. Away with you! You are but a hoodlum who makes out that he is strong. Next to love, you are a weakling. No matter how you may have buttressed my heart, my heart is fortressed with God. Next to God's love, you are but a broken matchstick. You are not going to start a conflagration in my heart! No, you're not!"

"And, so, you do not dance with this flimsy despair. You do not fall into his trap. Where did you ever get the idea that despair could overtake you? He can try. He can tap dance around you. You may be his prey, but you are definitely not his prize. He may try all his tricks, but you are immune to his charms, beloved. Despair has no place in your life. This dance is reserved for happiness.

"And so you ask Me, "Where is my happiness then? Where did it go? When will it come back?"

"Beloveds, your happiness is right here where it always has been. Despair cast a shadow over it, and soon the sun will come out, and the shadow will move as shadows must. Happiness never left. It was occluded from view by a shady character, no more than a scoundrel. No matter how renowned this scoundrel, scoundrels go away, and you will know happiness again."

From heavenletters.org 11/09/08

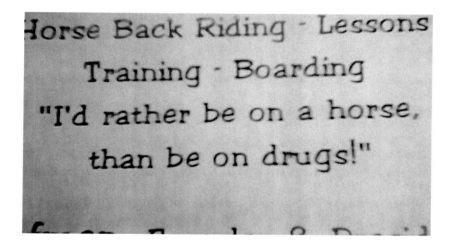

Horse Back Riding - Lessons
Training - Boarding
"I'd rather be on a horse,
than be on drugs!"

Footprints

One night, I had a dream.

I dreamed I was walking along the beach with the Lord, and across the sky flashed scenes from my life. For each scene,

I noticed two sets of footprints, one belonged to me and the other to the Lord.

When the last scene of my life flashed before me, I looked back at the footprints in the sand. I noticed that many times along the path of my life there was only one set of footprints. I also noticed that it happened at the very lowest and saddest times in my life.

This really bothered me and I questioned the Lord about it. "Lord, you said that once I decided to follow you, you would walk with me all the way, but I have noticed that during the most troublesome times in my life there is only one set of footprints. I don't understand why in times when I needed you most, you should leave me."

The Lord replied, "My precious, precious child, I love you and would never leave you. During your times of trial and suffering, when you saw only one set of footprints, <u>it was then that I carried you.</u>" - Mary Stevenson

Only one week after the roses incident, which you will read about next, I was once again praying, asking St Therese to intercede for me. I asked her to allow me to see Chris one last time, if it was God's will, to forgive face to face. To make amends.

That chance came at a book signing in his own town. I had just settled in when I saw his car drive by the window. Going to the door, I saw him stroll in. "Hi, Chris," I said with a smile. I hadn't seen him for three weeks. He looked good, yet was dressed all in black. He even wore dark sunglasses. It was a cloudy day outside, yet he never removed them even while in the building. All a part of that dark persona that he carried. I could feel the evil emanating from him. "uh, oh, what now?" I asked myself.

I remained calm, though inwardly, I wondered of the fury of his storm.

"Don't talk, just listen!" he said, pointing his finger at me, much like a parent, chiding a child. "You thought I was going to be a coward and not show up today, well, here I am!" He then proceeded to ream me out right in front of everyone, calling me names I can't even print here. As the torrent of hate filled the air, I didn't even flinch. I didn't get angry. I listened as he ranted how he was going to take me down professionally, that I was worthless, a slut! He then left, as did the other patrons who overheard his diatribe. I felt so embarrassed as my greatest fears were put on parade for all to hear.

There went my book signing, for no one else showed up that day.

Oh well, there also was the answer to my request. I had the face to face opportunity I had prayed for and he blew it big time, by not even granting me a chance to say anything. He thought I'd crumble, but like a lady, I stoically endured it. I never even cried later, for I had my answer. He didn't want reconciliation, preferring to bathe in his wounds.

After the book signing, I went to his place, once more, one last time. He was pacing his living room, as soon as he saw me in the window, he grabbed the phone.

"I'm calling the police!" he yelled at me. "You're trespassing!"

At that point, I gave up. It was no use. His paranoia was the straw that broke the camel's back. I left for good.

God said:

"You can know that I do understand the paces you go through. I understand your heartaches and that you have them. I know how it is, and yet I do not commiserate. I do not pat you on the back and say, "There, there." I do not say, "You poor thing."

"I straighten up your backbone. I say, "Keep going. Keep going." I say, "Pick yourself up. Rub the dirt off your scraped knee, and stand up."

"If you were Rocky, the boxer, and you were knocked down even for the tenth time, I would say to you, "Get up."

"No matter what might knock you off your feet, I would say to you, "Get up."

I would not waste your heart nor Mine on commiseration. I would not say, "Stay down until you feel better." I might say, "Take a few moments, catch your bearings, and now get up and stand upright." I would ask you not to be laid low. I would say, "Rise high."

Do not interpret this as to mean that I lack compassion. What else is there to say to you but to get up? And to get up again and again?

"You perceive that you have been knocked down. No matter how many punches you may have felt, the punches do not have the say over you. The blows do not have to be the traction for your life. However life may seem to deal with you, it is not to hold you down. You must get up, beloveds. You are someone who makes his way in life. You are a hero, and you do as heroes do.

"No matter how many ribs may have been broken, heroes get up anyway. And if they have broken legs, heroes may have to lie down for a while, but their minds and hearts have gotten up long before their legs can walk. Even immobile, they are marching. Heroes are undaunted. And so must you be.

"On a scale of virtues, pity ranks low, and self-pity ranks very low. Pity is a time-waster. It is staying in place. It really is no comfort. It has no virtue at all.

"Sometimes you may have a toothache, and your tongue keeps moving over the tooth, and I suppose there is a certain comfort every time the tongue touches the pain, but is it comfort or is it rather fascination? Be fascinated instead with the idea of getting out from where you may be feeling sorry for yourself.

"When you were a child and fell off your bike, you got up and rode it again. No one would have said, "Bad bike. What a dreadful thing happened! You poor thing. Don't ride your bike again. You have been damaged. Walk, don't ride from now on."

"Think of what a world this would be if no one felt sorry for himself or for another. Then people would begin to show their worth. They would begin to see their worth themselves. There would be no wounded, for everyone would get up. In the getting up is the healing.

"You have a reserve of strength, and it does not get used up. You are strong, and you are resilient, beloveds. You have strength of character. You have strength of determination. You don't stay down. You get up. You pull yourself up, and you pull the world with you. You throw off burdens. What was once does not have to be now."

heaven letters.org 11/15/08

Epilogue

I know that what you have just read has been, at times, brutal. It also has been filled with every other type of emotion that you can imagine, I relived that pain in writing this and it was not easy. Anger, sorrow, guilt, passion, the memories of the three men that I will always hold in my heart, despite the hurt they caused me…it has not been an easy journey. I apologize if the words offended you, but were necessary to describe, in accurate detail, what really happened. Nobody said that the path to recovery is easy or will be over with in a "short while." It is hard, it is filled with setbacks and pain and sorrow, which only fosters that vicious cycle of drinking/drugs to medicate from all the pain! I would not mislead anyone- because denial is the devils' advocate! I, too, have been there and done that! I know what you're thinking…"but you're famous! You have the perfect life!"

Well, no, I am just one of you, I still bleed red and I put on my pants one leg at a time. However, I have put my own reputation on the line that yes, author Diane Ganzer was and is… just one of us. That I have crashed to the bottom, but finally come back up, bruised, scarred, but ready to start over fresh. Indeed,

I look back and wonder that if only I had tried harder, longer, better, maybe those relationships I had would have been better, loving …lasting!

Then the tears flow because I know I have done enough. I have been forgiven.

It was early one Sunday morning, that I was on my hands and knees, scrubbing the kitchen floor and praying. The thoughts were overwhelming and I cried. I stood up and went before my statue of St. Therese, the Little Flower saint. I looked at her solemn face, thinking about the road ahead of me and asked her to send me a shower of roses, to let me know that I was doing the right thing in so many areas of my life. I cried again as I went about my work. I thought for sure that I was going to go insane. I could feel the devil's unrelenting taunt.

That afternoon, I took Theresa, my daughter, and her friend Sandy to the zoo. It was a cold day in November, yet I desired to be out and about.

As we walked into the conservatory, I admired the sounds of birds singing, the water rushing in the ponds, as well as the warmth and humidity. Theresa took pictures high and low with her cell phone as I lived in the moment.

On the way back to my car, I noticed something I hadn't noticed before when I pulled into the parking lot. Just across from my car was a small landscaped plot.

In it were roses- in full bloom.

Not just one or two.

There were many.

I smelled them one by one.

Then it hit me.

The roses I had asked for.

It had been very cold the past week, with nighttime lows below freezing.

This was Minnesota. And yet, the roses were in full bloom here.

It was nothing short of a miracle.

Can God give us any less of Himself?

The next day, out of the blue, I received this e-mail message:

Dear God,

The lady reading this is beautiful, classy & strong, and I love her. Help her live her life to the fullest. Please promote her and cause her to excel above expectations. Help her to shine in darkest places and love where it is impossible to love.Protect her at all times, lift her up when she needs you the most, and let her know that when she walks with you she will always be safe.

In Jesus' name.

Amen.

"Ask, and it shall be given."

What has resulted from the severing of my friendship and working relationship with Chris was being available for Guy to write his story and the successful story of Changing Gaits and how it saved MY life. As you have read, I have traveled down that road, the one that lead to despair. I am so glad that I found the narrow road at Changing Gaits, the one that leads to eternal life. I feel so humbled that little me was called upon to take on this endeavor, that God loves and trusts me enough to do this. I have been blessed and I will pass that blessing on to others in all that I do. It is with that belief that I hope you do not judge me harshly.

My one request is this: If you feel, as I do, that Changing Gaits is truly a deserving ministry that is doing, as Mother Teresa says, "small things with great love," then allow that feeling to permeate inside of you, and then, act on that feeling. Whatever it is, be it to donate to this very wonderful cause your time, talent or treasure, any and all of it will be so greatly appreciated. You will also be blessed for the gift that you have given, namely, the gift of hope that others may also be healed as I was, through the gift of a horse.

Thank you, Shadow and may God bless you!

And thank you, Lord…for saving Shadow's life…

And Guy's…

And mine……

And so many others, seen…and yet to come…..

Guy and Diesel

Shadow oversees the work that Guy is doing at CGI

"Celebrate yourself every day. Do honor to the life you have been given. It is yourself that God wants you to celebrate, not so much events. Events are of the past, and you are everything. You count. The past is long gone, and you are right here. Celebrate now, beloveds.

Celebrate this minute as we sit down together and talk about life, and what it is, and what it means to you. You may not grasp what life is. You may not be able to, yet you know that life means a lot to you, and the puzzle of your own life means a lot to you. This is the springtime of your life."

Acknowledgements

It would only be fitting to mention all of those for whom Changing Gaits would not be possible. These servants of God, past and present, are the ones responsible for setting out the path that has brought victory to so many people, to allow them to touch another's life in a positive way. Without them, the threads in a beautiful tapestry of love, we would not have a blanket of warmth. So here it goes. If we have missed anyone, it was NOT intentional, just know that in the hearts of many, you also are loved, prayed for and thought of!

Christopher Kaufman- Guy's son

Amanda Kaufman- Guy's daughter

Rachel Lund & Bruce- Rachel is the Executive Director for Changing Gaits

Amy Jo & Charlie Rothbauer

Andria Koefed

Ann Marie & Shawn Decker

Annette Rivard

Barb Stone & Josh Olson

Bob Bohnen

Bob and Jeannie Herzog

Bob & Sandy Rothbauer

Brian & Suzie West

Brooke Engen Goss

Carol & Don Koefed

Candy Lee

Cheryl Shanahan-Julian

Chuck Hills

Clovis & Jimmy Brackins

Coni Verhey

Dave & Judy Edditsvold

Dave Hall & Mary

Deb Colmer

Deb Rod

Deb & Ron Samuelson

Denise Kaufman- Guy's most industrious sister! She wears many hats…very well!

Don Gunderson

Donna Mozey

Doug & Jodi Kaufman

Doyne &Theresa Parsons

Ed &Linda Lewis

Eric Dewey & Family

Fred& Marti Carlson

Gary & Colleen Kislinger

George French

Glen & Dixi Schoenrock

Greg Hanson- board member

Greg & Paula Koalska- the foundation of Changing Gaits and board member

Hank & Cindy Magnuson- Wild River Stables...Shadow's home when he met Guy.

Jackie Hoover- current board member

Jeff Fossen, Jackie & Mackila

Jason Siems

John Jacobson

John Turner

Judy Curtis

Judy Smith

Ken,Vicki, Megan & Morgan Larson

Kevin Hoefed

Kim & Chris Pittman

Diane Ganzer

Ladonna Lafontain

Lanae, Bunny & Michelle Ross

Laurie & Jon Seebach

Lee & Patty Midlo- Country Camping Isanti, MN

Lisa Radkie

Liz Bilotta

Lori & Chris Moore

Lloyd Luloff

Lynn & Chris Moore

Lynn Thomas

Mary Brooks

Mason & Katie Marks

Melissa Colby

Marielle Robinson

Michelle Kaufman &Will

Mike Good

Mike &Tim Mehner

Mike Ryan

Mike & Shelly Widhelm

Mike & Shelly Westfall

Misty Smith

Pastor Mike Flynn

Pastor Howard Mcray

Paul Ridgeway

Paula & Jerry Price

Rachel & Bruce Lund

Rosemary & Tommy Novak Smith

Ruben Rosario- St Paul Pioneer Press reporter

Sandy Schaber

Scott's Tires

Shane & Mikki Heart

Shane Kaufman

Shelly and Will Kaufman

Skip [David] Bidney

Steve Halls

Terry & Katie Parsons

Tim Koran

Todd & Ann Schilling

Tom & Sandy

Tommy

Vera

Wendy Schuster

Will Barno

Last, but most definitely not the least, is Guy's own mother, Bonnie Kaufman. The sweetest lady you will ever meet. If not for the life she provided, Guy would not be here today. In fact, Guy almost was just a memory; Bonnie almost miscarried him when she rode on the Tilt-A-Whirl. As you can see, even from the start, it was predestined that Guy had a very special mission to fulfill, and God saw to it that it was done.

We all are a part of ministry, all we need to do is to ask God to help us discern just what it is…..

May you be blessed.

Alleluia!

www.changinggaitsinc.com

320-679-4468

"Do small things with great love…" Mother Teresa

Printed in the United States
221534BV00001B/2/P